Th

American Inventor

By Michael W. Simmons

Copyright 2016 by Michael W. Simmons

Published by Make Profits Easy LLC

Profitsdaily123@aol.com

facebook.com/MakeProfitsEasy

Table of Contents

Chapter One: Childhood and Early Life 4

Chapter Two: Edison the Entrepreneur 24

Chapter Three: The Phonograph 38

Chapter Four: Lights 72

Chapter Five: Edison in Manhattan 101

Chapter Six: Edison Reborn 129

Chapter Seven: Edison At War 164

Chapter Eight: The Edison Name 199

Appendix A: Edison's Employment Exam 224

Further Reading 240

Chapter One: Childhood and Early Life

"During all those years of experimentation and research, I never once made a discovery. All my work was deductive, and the results I achieved were those of invention, pure and simple. I would construct a theory and work on its lines until I found it was untenable. Then it would be discarded at once and another theory evolved. This was the only possible way for me to work out the problem. ... I speak without exaggeration when I say that I have constructed 3,000 different theories in connection with the electric light, each one of them reasonable and apparently likely to be true. Yet only in two cases did my experiments prove the truth of my theory. My chief difficulty was in constructing the carbon filament. Every quarter of the globe was ransacked by my agents, and all sorts of the queerest materials used, until finally the shred of bamboo, now utilized by us, was settled upon."

From "Talks With Edison", February 1890

Family

Thomas Alva Edison was born on the 11th of February, 1847, in Milan, Ohio, the youngest and last of Nancy Elliott Edison and Samuel Ogden Edison's seven children. Child and infant mortality rates in the mid-nineteenth century were so high that by the time of young Thomas's birth, only three of his siblings were still living. There was an age gap of more than a decade between Edison and his older sisters and brother, and all of them left home when Edison was still a young boy. As a consequence, Edison grew up more or less an only child, the sole subject of his parents' attention.

Nancy Elliott was born in upstate New York in 1808 or 1810, making her 18 or 20 when she was married to Samuel Edison. She was trained as a schoolteacher, unlike her husband, who had no formal education. Elliott moved to Ontario, Canada, with her father, Captain Ebenezer Elliott, where she met Samuel Edison in 1828. Her living children, beside Thomas, were Marion, William, and Harriet; the three children who did not live to maturity were Carlisle, Samuel Jr., and Eliza.

For a man who was to become one of the original American icons, Edison was descended on his father's side from a family that had never been particularly sold on the idea of America. His forbears were Dutch settlers who had immigrated to New Jersey, and who pronounced the family name as "EE-dison", with the long vowel sound in the first syllable. The Edisons were resident in New Jersey until the time of the American Revolution; according to biographical notes by Samuel Edison, his father John was "a stalwart Continental". In fact, John Edison—who may have been Thomas Edison's great-grandfather, rather than his grandfather—was a British Loyalist, a fact which seems to have embarrassed his descendants. Samuel Edison maintained that John Edison had fought in the Revolution, and only moved to Nova Scotia, Canada, after the war, to pursue business interests. In fact, John Edison, like many Loyalists, moved to Canada shortly after the Revolution *began;* the only member of the Edison family who participated in the war on the American side was a great-uncle who served as a secretary in the first Continental Congress.

After Thomas Edison became famous, reporters and writers from all over the world expressed interest in his pedigree, and Edison accordingly began to research his own genealogy. Having only his father's unreliable anecdotes to guide him, Edison made several errors in his research. The earliest biographies of Edison's life printed those errors as fact, without bothering to orate them with research, which is why ere is now some confusion about his ancestry. It is understandable, perhaps, that the American public preferred to believe that one of the most famous and beloved figures of their time was descended from Revolutionary-era patriots; by the time Edison became famous in the 1870's, the nation had scarcely celebrated its first centennial.

But if Edison's forbears missed out on one revolution, within a generation or two they became embroiled in another. Samuel Edison was born in Nova Scotia in 1804. He was not trained in a career, but worked various odd jobs in his life, from repairing roof shingles to keeping a tavern. He married Nancy Elliott when he was 24. Of their seven children, the elder four were all born in Ontario, and the family remained in residence there until ten years before Thomas Edison's birth. Then, in 1837, Samuel Edison became involved in the

Mackenzie Rebellion, or the Rebellion of Upper Canada, a populist democratic uprising against the oligarchic Canadian government. Samuel Edison had a keen interest in politics and consumed the writings of American philosopher Thomas Paine, which may have fueled his interest in participating in a rebellion that sought to import American democratic principles of government to British-ruled Canada. The Mackenzie Rebellion was quickly put down, and because of his involvement Edison was forced to flee to the United States to avoid prison. He ended up in Ohio, where his wife and children joined him in Milan once he was settled. In this manner, Thomas Edison was born as an American citizen, unlike every other member of his family apart from his mother.

Childhood

Edison was a sickly child for many years, which prevented him from starting school until he was eight. The precise details of his health problems known, but he seems to have had at least a bout with scarlet fever, a dangerous but common childhood illness in the 19th century that killed many of its victims and often led to health problems later in life for survivors. In Edison's case, it may have damaged his hearing; he certainly had hearing problems as a child that only grew worse as he grew older. However—in a theme that repeats itself throughout the course of his biography—Edison told conflicting stories as to the reason for his deafness, which makes it difficult to know how severe his early hearing problems were.

Edison attended a school run by a private instructor, a Reverend G.B. Engle. Edison did not have much success as a student under Engle's tutelage. Whether because of his hearing problems, or because he suffered from attention deficit disorder, or because he was dyslexic, the young Edison struck Engle as being "addled", a word which in the 19th century usually meant mentally ill or developmentally delayed. Engle expressed this opinion in a letter to Edison's mother, which angered her deeply and prompted her to remove her son from Engle's school and begin teaching him at home.

There is a popular story about this incident which has become part of the Edison legend. It claims that Edison was present when his mother read Engle's letter, and that when Edison asked her what the letter said, she claimed that his teacher had written that her son was a genius, and that she should teach him at home because the school was too small for him, and there weren't enough teachers to give such a promising pupil the attention he needed. Supposedly, after his mother's death, Edison was going through her papers and discovered the letter's true contents, leading him to remark that he owed all of his genius and invention to his mother's belief in him. This story is almost certainly untrue, because Edison was undoubtedly aware that

...sidered him to be slow; he often ...uted the anger he felt over this appraisal of ...is abilities to have motivated his efforts to make a success of himself. It is true, however, that Edison felt that he owed his start in life to his mother's patient teaching and her commitment to nurturing his early curiosity and love of learning. This story is just one example of how Edison's legend became peppered with sentimental anecdotes of dubious provenance, a byproduct of the extraordinary fame he later achieved and the public appetite for any sort of detail about his life.

When Edison became famous, his celebrity reached levels previously unknown in popular culture, and his life became legendary. This due partly to his many groundbreaking inventions, but it was also due to the fact that Edison fit a very specific biographical narrative that was wildly popular in America in the 19th century (and is, to some extent, still in vogue today): that of the self-made man from humble beginnings who was denied a formal education but achieved success regardless, owing to his efforts to educate himself. Edison was certainly an autodidact. Nancy Elliott's training as a school teacher enabled her to give her son a thorough grounding in reading, writing, and arithmetic, and Samuel Edison's political passions meant that he was able to introduce the young Thomas to the writings of important thinkers such as Thomas Paine. But it was not long before Edison's parents had taught him everything they knew, and he was left alone to work his way through the contents of his parents' library. It was a decent library, and Edison was more motivated than the average child to take advantage of it. He was much less fond of history and literature than he was of books about science and mathematics, but his father offered him a bribe of 10 cents every time he finished a novel or a history book. With this incentive to guide him, Edison cultivated a deep fondness for English literature; and it is amusing to consider

...inancial rewards played in his early ...ion, considering that his later fame was a ...sult of his business dealings almost as much as his inventive genius.

Whether it was his own restless nature that drove him, or whether the young Edison was inspired by his father's perpetual financial difficulties—he often had trouble making ends meet to support his family—Edison's earliest ambitions seems to have centered around making money. Indeed, this is what would set his career apart from that of dreamy visionaries like Nikola Tesla, or theorists like Einstein; Thomas Edison's original drive was to make money and be his own boss, and his facility for invention was simply the tool he used to make his businesses profitable. When Thomas was seven, Samuel Edison moved his family to Port Huron, Michigan, in search of work opportunities; as soon as he was old enough to be hired, Thomas persuaded his mother to let him apply for a job as a "newsboy" on a train that made frequent trips from Port Huron to Detroit. At the age of 12, Edison became the youngest importer of green groceries, dairy products, and dry goods in the state. He purchased fresh fruits, vegetables, butter, cheese, and other delicacies from Detroit, and transported them on the train back to Port Huron, where people were willing to pay Edison's markup to save themselves the price of the train trip to the big city. (The conductors and engineers aboard the train were Edison's first customers, which probably saved his business from getting shut down before it could get started.)

Edison's career as a junior train attendant lasted until he was sixteen, and he made the most of his educational and entrepreneurial opportunities during those years. By the time he was fifteen he had started his own newspaper, written, printed, and distributed entirely on board the train. This was during the middle of the Civil War, when traveling to larger cities meant that Edison got an earful of the latest news from the battlefields before anyone at home, enabling him to effectively scoop the very mainstream newspapers he was technically employed to sell. At the same time, Edison was running a small chemistry laboratory out of one of the empty train cars, where he performed small scientific experiments; these experiments, and his employment on the railway, came to an abrupt end one day, when some of the volatile chemicals he was working with spilled and ignited the train car. Reportedly, the conductor literally threw Edison out of the train by his ears, or possibly just boxed them—another potential reason for Edison's increasing deafness as an adult.

A new career

When Edison was fifteen, he found a mentor in the person of James MacKenzie, a station master on the railway. Edison and MacKenzie met when Edison spotted MacKenzie's toddler son playing on the train tracks in the path of an oncoming freight car. Edison made a run for it and pulled the child to safety, and in gratitude, MacKenzie began to give Edison his first lessons in Morse code, the kinetic language of dashes and dots used to relay telegraph message. Edison proved a quick study, and he was given a job at the station as a telegraph operator until a second nearly disastrous incident occurred. The teenage Edison was sent to stop a train that was on a collision course with another car on the same track. The train was traveling faster than Edison anticipated, however, and it passed him by before he could flag it down. He telegraphed the bad news down the line, and raced on foot to the next station, hoping to reach the station master in time to avoid a crash. Luckily for him and everyone else, the engineers of the two trains spotted each other and were able to brake in time to avoid a collision. But afterwards, MacKenzie was left with the awkward job of explaining why a sixteen year old boy had been entrusted with such an important and dangerous job, and Edison was threatened with arrest for criminal negligence. Rather than sticking around to find out if the superintendent intended to make good on that threat, Edison boarded the next train out of town.

It was the not particularly promising beginning of a new phase in Edison's career. He became a freelance, or rather, itinerant telegraph operator, one of a stable of young, unmarried men who roamed the country, working from different locations, bunking together and engaging in friendly competitions of telegraphy prowess. Taking and transmitting accurate telegraph messages was a stressful, fast-paced job. Edison was competent at sending telegrams, but he excelled at taking them down, translating Morse code to English quickly and without errors. He even experimented with his handwriting to find the fastest, most efficient method of transcribing messages legibly; the secret turned out to be writing in print, rather than in cursive longhand.

Soon he was entrusted with receiving longer, more important messages, such as stories transmitted by journalists to be printed in newspapers. One of Edison's early biographers thus describes the eclectic society into which Edison was thrown during this period:

"The young men who thus floated about the country from one telegraph office to another were often brilliant operators, noted for speed in sending and receiving, but they were undisciplined, were without the restraining influences of home life, and were so highly paid for their work that they could indulge freely in dissipation if inclined that way. Subjected to nervous tension for hours together at the key, many of them unfortunately took to drink, and having ended one engagement in a city by a debauch that closed the doors of the office to them, would drift away to the nearest town, and there securing work, would repeat the performance. At one time, indeed, these men were so numerous and so much in evidence as to constitute a type that the public was disposed to accept as representative of the telegraphic fraternity; but as the conditions creating him ceased to exist, the "tramp operator" also passed into history. It was, however, among such characters that Edison was very largely thrown in these early days of aimless drifting, to learn something perhaps of their nonchalant philosophy of life, sharing bed and board with them under all kinds of adverse conditions, but always maintaining a stoic abstemiousness, and never feeling other than a keen regret at the waste of so much genuine ability and kindliness on the part of those knights errant of the key whose inevitable fate might so easily have been his own."

The "abstemiousness" to which this passage refers is a reference to the fact that Edison, though addicted to nicotine, never drank alcohol, an extremely rare form of abstention in the mid-nineteenth century, long before the temperance movement raised public awareness about the dangers of immoderate alcohol consumption. In fact, Edison's aversion to alcohol was a considerable boon to his career. Not only did it mean that the time his fellow "tramp operators" spent carousing was time he spent studying and working on his inventions, but it made his employers, and even his coworkers, see him as a young man who was more likely to be honest and dependable than the rest of his peers.

Edison continued his efforts at self-education during this phase of his life, reading the works of English scientist and pioneer in electricity, Michael Faraday. Telegraph operators were responsible for maintaining their own telegraphy equipment, and Edison studied the battery operated receivers extensively, making notes on how the transmitters and receivers could be improved. These were his first forays into original inventions, and he would spend most of the next decade engrossed in the business of making telegraph equipment more efficient.

In 1868, when Edison was 19, he obtained a job with Western Union, the premier telegraph company of the 19th and early 20th century. He continued working on his own inventions, and by the age of 21 he had acquired a few investors who were interested in backing his projects, trading business capital for a share in any patents. This was, in fact, the year that Edison filed his first patents, including one for a device that would electronically tabulate votes in Congress and in state legislatures. Unfortunately for Edison and his investors, politicians refused to adopt this technological marvel—the old, slow process of counting votes by hand allowed the legislators extra time to talk amongst themselves and lobby for more votes. Such a device was of value to stock traders, however, who saw advantages in being able to communicate quickly, and would pay for equipment that allowed them to do so.

Edison saw a lucrative career in developing communication solutions for businessmen, and therefore, in 1869, he quit his job at Western Union and embarked on a life of full-time entrepreneurship. He was then 22 years old. By the age of 30, he would be a household name; by the age of 35, he would be one of the first genuine American celebrities, more famous than any other American, except perhaps George Washington and Abraham Lincoln, had ever been.

Chapter Two: Edison the Entrepreneur

Early business ventures and marriage

From 1869 to 1871, Edison was in the business of developing communication technologies. He regarded being in business for himself as the first condition necessary to his work—he needed to be his own boss and set his own schedule and make the sole decisions regarding the direction of his research. Fortunately for him, Edison had a talent for attracting the investors that would make this kind of autonomy, valued by all inventors but attained by few of them, possible. He had a number of different businesses under different names during this period, including Pope, Edison & Company, Edison & Unger, and Edison and Murray. He didn't enjoy unqualified success straight out of the gate—he sometimes despaired over paying his small stable of employees their wages, and grew frustrated by the tedious work of managing a business, preferring to devote his time to invention. But overall, his entrepreneurial efforts did fairly well for themselves, and he suffered no serious business disasters in his early career.

In 1871, Edison made the acquaintance of a young woman named Mary Stilwell, who was employed by Edison's News Reporting Telegraph Company, a company Edison had formed to sell private telegraph and printer access to the business world. This venture was not one of Edison's greater successes, but it brought him, at the age of 24, into the orbit of his future wife, who was then 15. Edison reportedly encountered Stilwell for the first time while she was "punching perforations into telegraph tape". The following excerpt, from one of the early biographies written about Edison, describes their peculiar first conversation, in which Edison apparently elected to propose marriage before bothering to ask her name:

"Among the young women whom he employed to manipulate these machines, with a view to testing their capacity for speed, was a rather demure young person who attended to her work and never raised her eyes to the incipient genius. One day Edison stood observing her as she drove down one key after another with her plump fingers, until, growing nervous under his prolonged stare, she dropped her hands idly in her lap, and looked up helplessly into his face. A genial smile overspread Edison's face, and he presently inquired rather abruptly:

"'What do you think of me, little girl? Do you like me?'"

"'Why, Mr. Edison, you frighten me. I—that is—I—'"

"'Don't be in any hurry about telling me. It doesn't matter much, unless you would like to marry me.'"

The young woman was disposed to laugh, but Edison went on: "'Oh, I mean it. Don't be in a rush, though. Think it over; talk to your mother about it, and let me know as soon as convenient—Tuesday, say. How will Tuesday suit you, next week Tuesday, I mean?'"

Mary Stilwell would later tell a different version of her first encounter with her future husband, claiming that she met Edison for the first time after she and her mother ran into his factory to take shelter from a sudden rainstorm. Perhaps the rainstorm incident happened before she was hired, and Edison simply forgot it. Stilwell certainly wasn't embarrassed by the fact that she had once been her husband's employee; she was a great favorite among the men who worked at

Edison's laboratories, because she had once been "one of them", and wasn't inclined to be snobbish about it now that she was married to the boss. In any event, Edison made a significant, if not overwhelming impression on her during their first meeting. She noted that "he had very handsome eyes...and he was so dirty, all covered with machine oil."

Stilwell was somewhat reluctant to accept Edison's advances at first, which hardly seems surprising considering the brusque way he introduced himself. But she permitted him to walk her home from work to meet her parents, and that introduction seemed to go better than the first. Stilwell's father knew who Edison was, being a lawyer and something of an inventor himself. With her parents' blessing, Mary began accepting visits from Edison, and after her sixteenth birthday, on December 25, 1871, they were married.

According to one anecdote, not even marriage managed to divert Edison's attention from his business interests and inventions for long. Edison returned to his laboratory immediately after his wedding, and when a friend found him still at his desk late that night, Edison asked him the time. On being told that it was midnight, he replied, "Is that so? By George, I must go home, then. I was *married* today."

The couple had a week long honeymoon in Boston before returning to New Jersey and setting up housekeeping in Newark. Mary Sitwell Edison was fortunate in that her husband had ample money to provide her with a new house, furnished to her taste, but less fortunate in other areas. Edison was not overly interested in domestic affairs, and usually failed to attend the dinner parties she hosted. But their marriage seems to have been a happy one overall, and their first child, a daughter named Marion, was born two years later, in 1873. Charmingly,

Edison nicknamed her Dot—as in, the dots and dashes of Morse code that are transmitted by telegraph wires.

Advances in telegraphy

Edison's chief interest in the early years of his career was in advancing telegraphy as a science. In the 1870's, no method of getting a message from place to place was faster than the telegraph—and it was the first means of relaying messages in all of history that was faster than carrying a message to its receiver on horseback. The telegraph had obviated the need for message delivery systems like the Pony Express; now Edison was searching for the technological advance that would make telegraphy obsolete. The speed at which a message traveled was no longer the chief barrier to improving communication. The problem now was sending two or more messages at once, rather than waiting for a single message to be transmitted and translated before the next one could be sent.

There was also a drive to automate the process—that is, to remove the need for skilled human operators to write down and translate the messages.

Edison tackled both of these problems, inventing a telegraph system connected to four wires, capable of sending four messages at once, and inventing an early forbear of the dot matrix printer to take down incoming telegraph messages. He was losing interest in these projects, which were largely pressed upon him by his investment partners; Edison wanted to devote himself to inventing in his laboratory full time. But he had an excellent relationship with his investors, or at least he never failed to impress them: upon being told that Edison had devised a means of fully automating telegraphy, one of his partners replied, "If you should tell me you could *make babies by machinery*, I shouldn't doubt it."

Menlo Park

In the early 1870's, Edison moved his family from Newark to Menlo Park, New Jersey, where he set up a private laboratory and promptly invented an electric pen, yet another technological advance with the potential to make telegraphy obsolete. Mimeograph machines, in later decades, would be based on this technology, although its more enduring application was in the form of the first electric tattoo needle. Edison was making a great deal of money on the patent royalties he received for the electric pen, as well as for his automated telegraphy system, and as a result, the Edison family was fairly on the way to being wealthy by the time their second child was born in 1876. His name was Thomas Alva Edison, Jr., and Edison nicknamed him Dash, to match his sister's nickname of Dot.

Edison's home and laboratory at Menlo Park would later become world famous and host a museum dedicated to Edison's memory. But when the Edison family first took up residence there, Menlo Park was isolated and deserted, surrounded by empty countryside. The property had been intended for real estate development, but the project had gone bankrupt, and only the one house had been built; there weren't even any trees in the vicinity, although there were plenty of snakes rustling through the grassy fields. On a hilltop behind the family home lay a long white building, which Edison sometimes referred to as "the schoolhouse"; this was his laboratory, and he would go on to invent the phonograph there, drawing power from the nearby railway lines.

Some of the inventions Edison developed at the Menlo Park laboratory include duplicating ink and an electric-sheep shearing machine, but Edison regarded these as mere trifles. He was still committed to improving telegraphy, as was another famous American inventor of his era, Alexander Graham Bell. Interestingly, it was through both men's attempts at improving the telegraph that the telephone came to be invented. Harmonic telegraphy attempted to provide a means of sending multiple messages down a telegraph wire at once; Bell came to realize that acoustic telegraphy could convey, not just the dashes and dots of Morse code, but any sound at all, including the sound of a human voice. Edison soon picked up on this notion, and it was Edison who invented a clearer receiver for sound waves conveyed in this manner. Edison and Bell were both consistently working on improving telephonic machines up to the point when Bell won the race by perfecting his first working prototype; afterwards, they competed with one another in patenting improvements to the device.

Telephones were not initially conceived of as the instrument of spoken communication we use today. The first public telephone demonstrations involved playing music that was being performed in one location to a remote audience in another location, a sort of proto live radio broadcast. Edison foresaw that telephones would soon be able to facilitate instantaneous spoken communication, but this news did not thrill everyone. As one newspaper reporter commented, "what an instrument of torture [the telephone] would be in the hands and the mouth of a distant and irate mother-in-law." Several inventors were in the business of improving the telephone for use as a transmitter of music, but the marketability of the musical telephone was hampered by the fact that such a device could only convey music that was being performed live. There was certainly a demand for such performances—audiences in New Jersey were willing to travel a few miles to pay for the privilege of listening to a concert that was taking place in New York, since it beat the trouble and expense of traveling to a far off city—but the real need was for music on demand, in other words, a machine that could play music that had been pre-recorded. It was in the process of trying to invent a telephone that could perform this feat that Edison ended up inventing the phonograph.

The secret to recording music proved to lie in the automated telegraphy system Edison had invented a few years earlier, the system that had removed the need for skilled human telegraph operators by replacing them with a printing machine that recorded signals using a stylus or needle and a strip of wax paper that ran beneath it on a sort of conveyor belt. At first, Edison had used this method to record voice messages sent by telegraph—messages that could be stored and translated from Morse to English at a cheaper and more leisurely rate than when telegraph operators received and translated messages simultaneously.

Edison often stayed at his laboratory all night working on a project, and when he stayed late, so did all of his employees. It was during one of these marathon night time work sessions that Edison came up with the idea that would give the phonograph shape: running a needle over the wax paper strips on which messages were recorded, then attaching the needle to a diaphragm (a thin membrane of suitable material, like a drumhead stood on its side, that transmits sound waves as vibrations). Speaking through the diaphragm would cause the needle to record onto the paper; running the needle over the paper would transmit the sound back through the diaphragm. The famous test phrase Edison used in this first recording experiment was, "Mary had a little lamb," from the children's nursery rhyme. According to those who observed the experiment, when the needle was set to play back the recording, the result sounded more like "ary ad ell am". The sound was not yet commercial quality, but the hypothesis had been proved by experiment. It only took Edison and his crew of midnight workers the rest of the night to produce a recording that was clear enough to be completely intelligible.

Chapter Three: The Phonograph

"...the Mania has broken out this way—Schoolgirls write compositions on Edison. The funny papers publish squibs on Edison. The religious papers write editorials on Edison. The daily papers write up his life...Why don't the Graphic fill up exclusively with Edison and done with."

> George Bliss, head of Edison's electric pen company

The Edison Speaking Phonograph Company

This first breakthrough on the phonograph came in July of 1877, but Edison was busy with other projects at the time and did not fully realize the potential of what he'd created until several months later. For a long time, the invention didn't even have an official name. Edison's right hand man, Charles Batchelor, initially referred to their new invention as a "Speaker telegraph," referring to its previous incarnation as a device for storing telegraph messages. And the initial focus was recording spoken messages; telephones were still seen as the proper instruments for playing music. Edison believed the phonograph would be principally useful as a means of taking dictation, or making voice memos. According to Edison biographer Randall Stross, one of Edison's employees came up with a list of potential names for the phonograph in which the word "phonograph"—which "was in common usage at the time as a synonym for 'shorthand'"—does not appear. The list is reproduced below:

> Tel-autograph
>
> Tel-autophone
>
> Polyphone = Manifold sounder
>
> Autophone = Self-sounder

Cosmophone = Universal sounder

Acoustophone = Audible speaker

Otophone = Ear-sounder = speaker

Antiphone = Back-talker

Liquphone = Clear-speaker

Chronophone = Time-announcer = Speaking clock

Didaskophone = Teaching speaker = Portable teacher

Glottophone = Language sounder or speaker

Climatophone = Weather announcer

Klangophone = Bird-cry sounder

Hulagmophone = Barking sounder

Omphlegraph = voice writer

Epograph = speech writer

Aerophone = air sound

Phonomime

Ecophone

Based on this list of potential names, two things seem clear: the Edison employee who made this list had access to a Greek dictionary, and he foresaw the technology behind the phonograph being developed for specialized use in a number of distinct market areas. The idea that the phonograph would be used primarily for musical recordings had not yet arrived on anyone's radar. Edison was interested in developing a kind of notated language that could be inscribed on wax paper and placed under a needle attached to a diaphragm and "read" aloud in perfect mimicry of human speech without any original recording being made, similar to the kinds of text-to-speech computer programs that are commonplace now. His investors were deeply interested in the progress of this invention, and advised Edison to keep it secret from his competitors.

It is difficult for modern readers to fully appreciate the impact that the mere concept of the phonograph had on the imaginations of people in 1877 when the secret finally got out. As Ross summarizes, people were "so excited—so emotionally moved...by the immediate prospect of being able to listen to the voices of the dead—that they jumped ahead to a list of possible applications of this new capability. Spoken messages might replace written letters. The words of history's greatest orators could be enjoyed in perpetuity. And 'music may be crystallized as well'." Such miracles are so commonplace to us today that it is almost impossible to imagine how revolutionary such notions seemed one hundred and fifty years ago. But it explains why the phonograph made Edison an instant worldwide celebrity when it was released: he had done something no one had ever imagined human beings would ever be able to do. Our present assumption is that technology has no real limits that time will not overcome, but in the 1870's, the world was a very different place.

Once word got out that the phonograph was being developed, via articles in magazines like *Scientific American*, the world began beating a path to Edison's door, demanding a working prototype. By early December of 1877, Charles Batchelor was referring to the invention as a "phonograph" and from that point forward the name seemed to stick. Edison was beginning to grasp that his machine might enjoy greater popularity as an entertainment device for music than for playing recorded messages; he imagined selling the phonograph with thousands of sheets of "pre-recorded music"—in other words, records—for buyers to enjoy at their leisure. He had not yet conceived than an industry would develop around the recording of music that would take record production out of the hands of the inventors and into the hands of musicians.

When Edison and two of his colleagues displayed the final working prototype of the phonograph for the first time, it was to the editors of *Scientific American* magazine. Edison had prepared a recording in which the phonograph essentially introduced itself: "How do you do? How do you like the phonograph?" it asked. The performance stunned Edison's small audience. Other attempts had been made at reproducing the human voice, but those devices were more akin to musical instruments, with pipes and rubber lips. The editors of the magazine could scarcely believe that it was possible to create such a lifelike sonic effect with a machine that was so small, and so unlike human vocal cords. The phonograph demonstration struck the editors as so important that the magazine delayed publication of its next edition by 24 hours to allow for a full write-up of Edison's visit. Below is a long excerpt from the original *Scientific American* article, published on

December 22, 1877, describing the impression the phonograph made on its first audience:

"Mr. Thomas A. Edison recently came into this office, placed a little machine on our desk, turned a crank, and the machine inquired as to our health, asked how we liked the phonograph, informed us that it was very well, and bid us a cordial good night. These remarks were not only perfectly audible to ourselves, but to a dozen or more persons gathered around[...]"

"No matter how familiar a person may be with modern machinery and its wonderful performances, or how clear in his mind the principle underlying this strange device may be, it is impossible to listen to the mechanical speech without his experiencing the idea that his senses are deceiving him. We have heard other talking machines. The Faber apparatus for example is a large affair as big as a parlor organ. It has a key board, rubber larynx and lips, and an immense amount of ingenious mechanism which combines to produce something like articulation in a single monotonous organ note. But here is a little affair of a few pieces of metal, set up roughly on an iron stand about a foot square, that talks in such a way, that, even if in its present imperfect form many words are not clearly distinguishable, there can be no doubt but that the inflections are those of nothing else than the human voice."

"We have already pointed out the startling possibility of the voices of the dead being reheard through this device, and there is no doubt but that its capabilities are fully equal to other results just as astonishing. When it becomes possible as it doubtless will, to magnify the sound, the voices of such singers as Parepa and Titiens will not die with them, but will remain as long as the metal in which they may be embodied will last. The witness in court will find his own testimony repeated by machine confronting him on cross-examination--the testator will repeat his last will and testament into the machine so that it will be reproduced in a way that will leave no question as to his devising capacity or sanity. It is already possible by ingenious optical contrivances to throw stereoscopic photographs of people on screens in full view of an audience. Add the talking phonograph to counterfeit their voices, and it would be difficult to carry the illusion of real presence much further."

From the moment this issue of *Scientific American* hit newsstands, Thomas Edison became, at the age of thirty, a celebrity superstar—biographer Randall Stross uses the word "superhero". Edison was flooded with requests by reporters for interviews and tours of his laboratories, and he chose to take a few journalists under his wing, treating them like friends, and letting them explore his workshop.

The journalists, who usually had no scientific or mechanical training, could only rely on Edison's explanations when it came to giving their readers a glimpse of his inventions, and Edison had a slightly mysterious manner that gave the impression that he had invented many things equally as astonishing as the phonograph which he simply had not yet revealed to the general public.

The following excerpt from an article published in the *New York World* in November of 1887 demonstrates Edison's showman-like ability to generate interest in his inventions by speaking of them as if they were slightly magical:

"Perhaps I am wrong in telling you anything about my phonograph, because what I claim for it is so extraordinary that I get only ridicule in return. I am so confident that when the apparatus appears it will dispel all doubts as to its practicability and working value that I can afford for the present to ignore all kinds of criticism and keep at my work regardless of the storm which I have been raising by telling a few people that there was such a thing as a perfected phonograph in existence. I am sure that while scientific men may doubt that I have succeeded as well as I say I have, they will admit that there is nothing at all impossible in what I claim, and that the germ of the perfected phonograph, should such a thing appear, is very clear in my old toy of ten years ago, which was exhibited all over the country, and was then acknowledged to be one of the wonders of the century. Just consider for a second what my old phonograph is, and think how little needed to be done to bring it to a working instrument. With my roughly constructed instrument of 1877 I reproduced all sorts of sounds, getting back from the phonograph something like the original sound. Of course, you had to yell into the thing, and the reproduction of conversation was often something of a caricature of the original.

Nevertheless, to obtain a result that could be understood was doing wonders, and most people who remember my exhibitions will admit that while I did not produce a commercial machine, I made a very interesting and creditable attempt, and my whistling and singing phonograph was a wonder.

"For music I know that you will simply laugh when I tell you what I have done with the two instruments that I have finished. I have got the playing of an orchestra so perfectly that each instrument can be heard distinct from the rest. You can even tell the difference between two pianos of different makes; you can tell the voice of one singer from another; you can get a reproduction of an operatic scene in which the orchestra, the choruses, and the soloists will be as distinct and as satisfactory as opera in this sort of miniature can ever be made. Opera by telephone has been done in Paris and London more or less successfully, but the phonograph will eclipse the telephone for this purpose beyond all comparison, and phonographic opera will cost nothing, because the phonogram can be passed through the phonograph, if necessary, a thousand times in succession, and once the machine is bought there is no other cost beyond the trifle for phonograms. For books the phonogram will come in the shape of a long roll wound upon a roller. To make the first phonographic copy of a book some good reader must of course read it out to the instrument; once that is done, duplication to any number of thousand or million copies is a simple mechanical work, easy and cheap. Now, just think for a moment what that means.

"Suppose you are sick, or blind, or poor, or cannot sleep. You have a phonograph, and the whole world of literature and music is open to you. The perfected phonograph is going to do more for the poor man than the printing press. No matter where he is, the poor man can hear all the great lecturers of the world, can have all the great books read to him by trained readers, can hear as much of a play or an opera as if he was in the next room to the theater, and all this at a cost scarcely worth mentioning. I remember that when the telephone was first announced it was said that now people in the wilds of Africa or America might assist nightly at the performances of the Paris Opera House. The wires from that favored spot might run to all parts of the world. Well, we have not yet got to that, though it is a scientific possibility for the future to perfect in detail. But the phonograph will make such a thing perfectly easy. The phonographic record of a performance at the Paris Opera House can be duplicated by the thousand and mailed to all parts of the world. I don't know but that the newspaper of the future will be in the shape of a phonogram, and the critic will give his readers specimens of the performance and let them hear just how the future Patti did her work, well or otherwise. This sounds like the wildest absurdity, and yet, when you come to think of it, why not?

Have I told you enough to make you believe that I am joking? Well, I am nothing of a joker, and this is all the most sober kind of statement. Within two months from now the first phonographs will be in the market."

Even after the world learned of Edison and the phonograph, he still had not come up with the idea of selling it as a home entertainment device for playing music. Rather, he began developing toys, like dolls and trainsets and stuffed animals, with small phonographic devices inside them that made them "talk". He wasn't sure that the average, every day consumer would ever see a use for the phonograph except as a toy. This was partly because the early phonograph was powered by a hand crank, which made playback inconvenient for records that lasted more than a few minutes.

Consumer marketing was not at all Edison's particular skill—he was accustomed to selling to clients in the business and industrial worlds. But he received an advance of ten thousand dollars from his investors to get a marketable prototype of the phonograph up and running. For once, Edison's backers had less than complete confidence in him—or at least, their eagerness to start making money off the phonograph made them especially anxious that Edison might spend all the money they had given him before the prototype was complete. In the end, Edison was so annoyed by the pressure to produce a commercial version of the phonograph as quickly as possible that he created a miniature, novelty version of the phonograph that could only record fifty words at a time, just so his investors would have something to release while he perfected the larger model.

"A marvelous invention"

Amos Cummings of the *New York Sun* came to visit Edison at his Menlo Park laboratory in February of 1878. He had been amongst the first reporters to get in contact with Edison after the first phonograph story appeared in *Scientific American*; Edison had promised him an interview, but as he got increasingly caught up in his work, he had put Cummings off, unwilling to travel to New York to talk to him. At last Cummings offered to come to New Jersey to see him, and Edison agreed to answer questions and let Cummings see the inside of his laboratory. The article that Cummings produced in response to this visit, while not solely responsible for catapulting Edison into fame, began to shape Edison's legacy as a kind of wizard or magician, capable of bending the barely-understood forces of scientific engineering to his will. Cummings' famous sketch of Edison from the opening paragraphs of the article demonstrates how he achieved this effect:

"Prof. Edison was seated at a table near the center of the room. He looked like anything but a professor and reminded me of a boy apprentice to an iron moulder. His hands were grimy with soot and oil; his straight dark hair stood six ways for Sunday; his face was entirely beardless but sadly needed shaving; his black clothes were seedy, his shirt dirty and collarless, and his shoes ridged with red Jersey mud; but the fire of genius shone in his keen grey eyes and his clean cut nostrils and broad forehead indicated strong mental activity. He seems always to be looking for something of great value and to be just on the point of finding it. Unfortunately he is quite deaf, but this infirmity seems to increase his affability and playful boyishness. A man of common sense would feel at home with him in a minute; but a nob or prig would be sadly out of place. Though but 31 years old, the occasional gleam of a silvery hair tells the story of his application."

When Cummings' story appeared in the *Sun*, it set off a public frenzy for more profiles of Edison. Menlo Park was near enough to New York by train that it was easy for reporters from the major papers to pop by for a visit, which they began to do in such large numbers that Edison complained to his attorney that he scarcely had time to invent, there were so many visitors in his laboratory. He made no attempts to forbid the visits, however; he understood the value of all the free publicity they were giving him.

Edison received a large volume of letters from people who had read about him in the newspapers, most of them admirers, some of them skeptics. One earnest professor of science tried to persuade Edison to contradict the claims he had made in the *Sun*. The professor assumed that the "scientifically impossible" inventions alluded to in Cummings' article had been made up, or at least wildly exaggerated into existence, by the reporter. He did not suspect Edison of any dishonesty, but he felt that Edison should distance himself from the article for the sake of his own credibility and reputation. The fact was, even though Edison was given to flippancy when speaking with reporters, he never made a claim that he didn't *think* he could back up. Some of the inventions he mentioned to reporters later proved unworkable, or never got past the planning stages due to the sheer volume of projects Edison had on his plate, but he believed in the potential of all his ideas and, at least at this stage in his career, did not intentionally misrepresent his capabilities.

One of the newspaper articles written about Edison during this period dubbed him "the Wizard of Menlo Park", and made his laboratory sound like a vast wonderland of unbelievable inventions. The nickname followed Edison throughout his life, even though he would move his base of operations away from Menlo Park in just a few years. Edison began to acquire such a fantastical reputation—"wizard" scarcely seemed like an exaggeration of his abilities, to judge by some of the articles that were written about him—that there seemed to be no limit to what a credulous public would believe about him. An article appearing in the *New York Daily Graphic* in April of 1878, entitled "A Food Creator", gave Edison credit for an invention that, unsurprisingly, boggled the minds of all who read about it. According to the reporter:

"A lunch was spread on a table, and [Edison's friend Edward Johnson] explained, 'Edison wished us to ask you to lunch here,' and sat down with me.

"What were we eating? This was the puzzle. There were several dishes. One was a solid, looking like head-cheese, but tasting like woodcock or some very delicate game. It was easily cut with a knife. Then there was soda biscuit with butter and honey. Coffee, too, or at least a warm beverage that looked like coffee, but had a delicious aroma, different from anything I had ever seen. The additional dish was a sort of Bavarian gelatin with cream and quince jelly poured over it—a flavorous dish. I inquired what had been set before us, but the Professor laughed and, hoping I would accept his assurance that it was harmless, said he must leave the explanation to Edison[...]

"Presently Edison came in, with a hurried stride and very breezy air... Edison took a hasty morsel, and lifting up a piece of the gamy substance on a fork, asked: 'Do you know what this is?' Receiving a negative answer, he continued:

"'The Graphic has been very generous in its descriptions and illustrations of my work. I am going to tell you something. I have a big secret. To-day I have got the receipt for my caveats from Washington and may safely tell you about it. I believe I have struck the biggest invention of this age. What do you suppose it is?'"

"'The phonograph,' I said.

"'Oh no, something new,' he replied.

"'Perpetual motion,' I suggested.

"'No,' he answered, ' a perpetual motion that is good for anything as a propelling power is, I believe, impossible. I have hit on something much greater than that. This food.'

"'This food?'

"'Yes—I made all these samples out of the dirt taken from the cellar and the water that runs through these pipes. I can make tons in the same way. The process is very cheap. And it is as simple as it is cheap. And it is capable of infinite variety.'

"I was dumb with awe as the possibilities of the new invention unfolded before me.

"'I believe—in fact, I know,' said he, rising and walking hurriedly around the room and tapping the partition and furniture with his fingers, as is his curious habit, 'that in ten years my machines will be used to provide the tables of the civilized world. Meat will no longer be killed and vegetables no longer grown, except by savages, for my method will be so much cheaper.'

'"What will become of the farmers, Mr. Edison?'

'"They will not need to drudge as they do now. The days of hard work are over. They can study and enjoy life.'

'"But how will they support themselves?'

'"You forget that men work chiefly to obtain food. When food costs them next to nothing, they will need to work only for shelter, clothes, and luxuries[…] All of our food comes primarily from the earth. The plants and fruits we eat come from the moist ground; and the animals we eat live on the plants or on other animals which the plants have kept alive. So all food comes from the elements that are stored up in earth, air and water. You eat a rain of wheat, for instance. That wheat is mainly composed of a few simple gases and salts that last year were lying dormant in the earth, the air and the water. It occurred to me that this process might be hastened; that, instead of waiting a year for nature to collect those elements into an organic seed, I could collect them in an hour, or perhaps a few minutes, and arrive at the same results by combining them inorganically. This I have done. '[...]

'"What is to be the result of your invention, Mr. Edison?'

'"Well, I think that after two or three years New Yorkers, for instance, will no longer eat meat or vegetables. They will not send to the tropics for fruits or to Europe for wines, because the head of every family, by turning a crank (or perhaps without turning a crank, if a clock apparatus is attached), can produce more

delicious fruit and wines at a tenth of the cost.'
[...]

"Your phonograph is going to abolish short-hand writers, and now this food-machine is going to dispense almost entirely with farmers and stock-raisers, with millers and bakers—why, it seems to me you are going to abolish all occupations except the manufacture of your machines.'

"Edison, laughing: 'Not quite. But this will certainly revolutionize the world. It will lighten toil. It will annihilate famine and pauperism. It will turn commerce inside out and upside down. It will do a vast deal of good, and, incidentally, it will cause some distress. But the world must take it for what it is worth. It is only an accident that I discovered it."

This fantastic newspaper article concludes:

> "At this point there came a rumbling in my ears, the breeze blew through the window upon my face and I awakened just in time to hear the conductor sing out, in a prolonged shout, *"Men-lo Park!"* And I rubbed my eyes and we bundled off the train to go and see the wonderful Edison."

Not only was the whole encounter a dream, but the publishing date of April 1st, 1878, probably ought to have clued the articles' readers into the fact that the story about Edison's "food creator" machine was only a prank, a satire on all the other articles about Edison that made him out to be capable of superhuman feats of invention. Edison, for one, thought the article was extremely funny. But many people, apparently having failed to read to the very end, took the article seriously. Edison was inundated with letters from people asking when the "food creator" would be ready for sale—the newspaper report indicated that it would only cost five or six dollars, after all. The fact that people found it plausible that Edison could have invented a cheap, simple machine that could create a fantastic variety of edible food out of dirt and water says a great deal about the sort of reputation Edison had already acquired. It also serves as a reminder of how the late 19th century public felt about the phonograph—to them, the idea that human beings could speak to a machine and hear the machine speak their words back to them seemed scarcely less baffling than the idea that several tons of food could be produced in a day by turning the crank on a small box.

Edison's reputation was made by the phonograph—or more accurately, by the *idea* of the phonograph. It is extraordinary to think that a person could become so famous on the strength of an invention that only a tiny handful of magazine editors and Edison employees had actually seen with their own eyes. Public demand for the phonograph was so intense that Edison's investors and business managers rather let their imaginations run away with them in planning the product launch—they envisioned selling the phonographs for $100, when they only cost $15 to make, and making customers pay the full price in advance before they were able to take the product home. Edison was not involved in that end of the business, but he was concerned that his investors were creating customer expectations that he could not help but disappoint. The plan was still to release a miniature, novelty version of the phonograph while the full model was still being developed. Edison felt that customers would find the "toy" version of the machine deeply dissatisfying, after all the claims that had been made about the original prototype. He suggested to his investors that customers be allowed to lease the toy model, but this suggestion was not well taken.

Surprisingly, fame did not make any immediate difference to Edison's life, apart from the fact that he was entertaining the occasional visit from newspaper reporters. Even these visits were not a great hindrance to his work—the biggest drain on his time and energy resulting from his celebrity was the enormous volume of mail he received. Being unaccustomed to the spotlight, he valiantly attempted to read and reply to almost every letter he received, including the ones from strangers who believed he was fabulously wealthy and could easily spare them a loan.

Edison was not fabulously wealthy, however, and he did not make very much money off the phonograph during the first ten years of its existence, largely because it took him that long to get a working full scale model ready for commercial sale. The only money he made off the phonograph before then was the royalty money he received from phonograph demonstrations. Edison had a few working prototypes of the phonograph which he sold to people who traveled around the country, giving demonstrations to the public in lecture halls and theaters; the performances succeeded in keeping the public interest in the phonograph keen, but they only netted Edison about a thousand dollars in royalty checks.

In April of 1878, Edison himself was given the opportunity to demonstrate the phonograph in Washington, D.C., before the National Academy of Sciences, an audience of the most influential scientific thinkers of the day. He did not particularly enjoy giving public demonstrations himself—showing off for reporters and visitors in his lab was one thing, but he disliked crowds and wasn't much of a performer. The president of the academy gave a flattering speech in Edison's honor, which Edison was not able to hear. But the trip to Washington wasn't a complete waste;

he was invited to the U.S. Naval Observatory, and was asked to give an impromptu, late night private phonograph demonstration to President Rutherford B. Hayes and his wife. Inventors and scientists throughout history have rarely received this kind of high-level recognition in their own lifetimes, but no doubt Hayes was just as curious as every other American about Edison and his inventions.

Chapter Four: Lights

"I don't care so much about making my fortune as I do for getting ahead of the other fellows."

Thomas Edison

The phonograph stalls

The reason it took Edison ten years to get a working prototype of the phonograph ready for the commercial market was mainly because he was distracted by his own creativity. He constantly pursued new avenues of invention, one burst of inspiration branching into three new projects, all of them equally promising. The reporters who profiled him for their papers often depicted Edison as the sort of absent-minded professor who cared only about discovery for discovery's sake, an unworldly creative genius whose brilliance translated to a sort of naiveté.

To a certain extent, this gloss on his character is accurate: he was preoccupied by his work to the point of distraction. Even though his laboratory was located only a few feet from his house, he scarcely set foot in it. He rarely took meals with his family or slept at home; 18 hour work days were normal for him and he often labored for days at a time without rest or food. Despite his propensity for distraction, however, he wasn't quite as unworldly as the papers made him seem. He certainly wasn't a Nikola Tesla, on a high-minded philanthropic quest to save the world with his inventions. He wasn't even interested in fame, except as a means to an end. Edison wanted to make money from his inventions; he had been an entrepreneur since he was twelve years old, after all. He just didn't want to bother his head about the boring details of business.

Edison wanted to invent at all hours of the day and night. There were always half a dozen new prototypes on his work table, waiting to be developed: a new kind of hearing aid that might enable him to work around his hearing impairment, a microphone that could replace the stethoscope in medicine, and others. He had carefully arranged the structure of his company to ensure his complete autonomy. His investors could plead with him to produce the phonograph, but they could not put pressure on him to do so.

But it is curious that Edison wasn't more intrinsically motivated to bring such a hotly anticipated product to commercial production, considering that he was so keenly interested in making money. Perhaps he believed, with some justification, that the eventual success of his inventions was assured, and the money was bound to come sooner or later. Or perhaps he was simply prone to the same weakness as many creative personalities—constantly seeking the next "eureka" moment, in which the secret of how an invention worked became clear to him in a flash of inspiration. If that was the case, it would go a long way towards explaining why he delayed the completion of the phonograph for so long. The phonograph's eureka moment had long since passed. All that was left was grinding out the details of making the invention suitable for mass production, work that must have seemed quite boring to him by comparison.

It would scarcely have been possible for Edison to become more famous than he already was, but after performing his phonograph demonstrations in Washington for the American Academy of Sciences and for President Hayes, he was positively hounded by visitors at his Menlo Park laboratories. Not only journalists, but interested strangers appeared on his doorstep, sometimes in groups of a hundred of more. Bemused observers suggested that he close his workshop to the public save on select days of the week, or else that he build an auditorium nearby so that visitors wouldn't be so underfoot. At times he lost an entire day's work to demonstrating the capabilities of the phonograph to these visitors; sometimes, he fled the laboratory entirely and left the demonstrations to his assistants.

Edison always had a complex relationship with his own fame. Though it had never been his goal to become famous, he was understandably flattered by the attention, particularly as it was almost universally positive. Nowadays, a person catapulted into unexpected celebrity tends to find that no sooner have they entered the public eye someone is waiting to find fault with their character, but the media was somewhat different in the 1870's. In the absence of television or radio, the public's only access to a celebrity figure was through the newspapers, and Edison cultivated his relationship with reporters carefully, making friends with them and treating them as valued guests. In return for this access to his life, they fueled public fascination with his inventions, which helped Edison make money.

From the moment he first became famous at the age of thirty, to his death five decades later, Edison managed to keep the American press eating out of his hand. But even as a beloved celebrity, Edison soon began to tire of the demands that celebrity made of him. A steady stream of visitors was driving him out of his own laboratory, and he was continuing to receive upwards of 80 letters a day from strangers. Not all of them were seeking autographs or loans. Edison's deafness, and his attempts to develop hearing aids and other adaptive equipment to ameliorate it, seems to have struck a chord with disabled persons all over the country. Many of his correspondents wrote begging him to invent devices that would help with their own infirmities, such as one man with vision problems who asked Edison to create a "blindoscope".

Edison goes west

Under pressure from these various forces—his impatient investors, reporters, uninvited visitors, and domestic concerns such as the approaching birth of his third child—Edison decided, suddenly, in July of 1878, to take a long trip west in the company of Professor George Barker. The pretext for the trip was an upcoming eclipse, which could be viewed to best advantage in Wyoming. From there, Edison would travel to California, and then back east to St. Louis, where he would present a paper to the American Association for the Advancement of Science.

Edison ended up extending his Wyoming visit into a tour of Montana, where he was taken on hunting expeditions into the wilderness by the locals, and, according to his own unverified account, came within a very narrow shave of being murdered by Ute Indians. From Montana he traveled to San Francisco, Yosemite, and Nevada; when he finally reached St. Louis, he was inducted into the American Association for the Advancement of Science as a member.

When Edison returned to Menlo Park, reporters and visitors were, as usual, awaiting his return, eager to claim some of his time. They asked for his impressions of the west, and whether he had enjoyed his trip, and then they asked him whether he had had any ideas for new inventions. In fact, Edison had conceived the idea for his most famous invention during his trip—the electric light—but he did not bother to share this information with the press just yet.

The invention of the electric light

Thomas Edison is, today, best remembered as the inventor of the electric light, but the truth is slightly more complex than that. Whenever one inquires into the history of an invention, one discovers that they rarely spring into existence from the mind of an inventor fully formed. The version of an invention that is best known and best remembered is usually the last in a series, and the versions that precede the final form are usually the work of a number of different people. So it was with the electric light. It would be more accurate to say that while Edison did not invent electric lighting, he invented an *efficient* incandescent electric light bulb that was fairly cheap, and was safe and suitable for use in private homes.

The history of the electric light begins in 1808, long before Edison's birth, when an Englishman named Humphry Davy first demonstrated that light could be produced in the form of an arc, by making a streak of controlled lightning jump from point A to point B, or incandescently, by heating a metal filament until it glowed brightly. But this was as far as the science of electric lights advanced until 1855, when Edison was still a young child, and electric arc street lighting was introduced in Lyon, France. The French public was treated to a spectacle mimicking artificial sunlight, so intensely bright that people had to shield their eyes with parasols and umbrellas. Regulating the intensity of arc-based electrical light was one of the biggest challenges faced by early inventors. The light it produced was brilliant and blinding, far too powerful to be used indoors. Incandescent lighting was far softer, but the problem there lay with finding a suitable metal to act as a filament. Some metals, such as carbon, burnt out too quickly, while others, such as platinum, were too expensive and too prone to melting. Such was the state of the electric light in 1878, when Edison returned from his trip to the American west with a head full of new ideas.

Finding a suitable power source for electrical lighting was one of Edison's principal challenges. Humphry Davy had used battery power, and batteries were still being used in most electrical lighting experiments, but Edison had grown interested in the potential of hydro power after viewing Niagara Falls. The real solution, however, presented itself when Edison was introduced to an electrical engineer in Connecticut by the name of William Wallace, who had built a dynamo, or electromagnetic generator, in his private laboratory. Wallace's dynamo was capable of sustaining arc lighting at the luminosity of 4000 candlepower, which was far too bright for indoor use, but the fault lay in arc lighting generally, not in Wallace's power source. Edison no sooner set eyes on the dynamo than he realized that he need look no further for a sustainable power source—all he needed to do now was create a filament that would make incandescent bulbs convenient and practical for home use, and electric lighting would become a facet of modern life.

Because Edison was so famous, and because he spoke his mind freely to the reporters he had become friends with, he scarcely seemed to have an idea for an invention that he did not mention offhandedly to a journalist, who then published it for the public to speculate about. He was no longer enjoying fame quite as much as he had in the beginning, but he certainly wished to maintain the public's interest in his inventions. Shortly after he returned from his trip west, he asserted to a journalist that he wanted to invent something just as original and groundbreaking as the phonograph every single year. It was an ambitious goal, and as it related to electrical lights, not entirely feasible—after all, a number of talented electrical engineers had worked on the problem of electric lights, whereas nothing like the phonograph had ever been imagined when it sprang into existence. (It is also a telling indication that, in Edison's mind, the phonograph ranked as a finished invention—even though his investors and the public were still waiting for a finished version to become commercially available.)

Edison had only been working on his electric light experiments for a week before he told a reporter that he had solved the problem, and that the solution was so simple that his fellow inventors would be kicking themselves when he showed the public how it had been done. Such was Edison's reputation that this announcement caused gas shares in London to drop almost immediately. There was just one problem: Edison had grossly overstated his progress, and was actually nowhere near a working solution. And while he wasn't given to making empty claims on purpose, he was so beset on every side by journalists that he could hardly make a thoughtless passing comment about his work without it being printed in the papers and taken as gospel.

Edison had begun his experiments by working with platinum filaments. The temperature at which platinum gave off incandescent light was dangerously close to the temperature at which it began to melt, so Edison attempted to build a mechanism that would stop the power feeding to the filament automatically when the temperature started getting too high. Temperature regulation had been attempted by many inventors before him and Edison had no more success than his predecessors. Rather than admit the delays he had encountered to the public, Edison set out to intentionally hoodwink them by inviting them to his laboratory to view a model incandescent bulb: it only worked for three minutes before heating to melting point, but he made sure to power it off before the reporters could witness that happening. When asked if he was having any difficulty with his new invention, Edison denied it point-blank. This may have been vanity on his part, but it was probably also due to the fact that investors were expressing interest in helping Edison form a company around his electric lights, and he needed them to remain confident in his work.

Edison Electric Light Company

The dip that British gas shares took as a result of Edison's precipitous claims about his success sparked a miniature crisis in the gas industry as a whole. In the 19th century gas companies constituted a highly unpopular monopoly on the utilities they provided, meaning they dictated the prices they charged and had no marketplace competition to undercut them. When Edison began to claim that he was close to inventing an electric light that could be used in private homes, newspaper reported ecstatically that if he could break the power of the gas monopoly, he would be more than a great inventor—he would be doing a service in the name of human decency. Edison had tangled with the gas companies himself when they threatened to cut off gas to his laboratory, and he confessed that he would not mind making things difficult for them. Gas company shareholders were divided as to whether Edison's lights actually posed a threat to them or not, but, tellingly, one of the principle investors in Edison's new Electric Light Company—to the tune of fifty thousand dollars—was William Vanderbilt, who owned enormous quantities of gas stocks.

But Edison was well aware that this funding would probably dry up if word got out that he was much further behind on his electric light than he had publicly claimed. For the first time, he closed the doors of his laboratory to the public, including reporters. Luckily for him, he had a ready-made excuse for this unprecedented display of inhospitality. The previous year, *Scientific American* had printed a story about the phonograph which included a complete diagram of the apparatus and a detailed analysis of how the machine worked. The story had been translated into French and German, and as a result, inventors all over the world were attempting to build phonographs for themselves.

Edison's partner Edward Johnson had tried to invoke patent law to stop anyone building phonographs based on these diagrams, but, as the editors of *Scientific American* pointed out, there was no legal basis for preventing an amateur from constructing a phonograph so long as they were using it for educational or other non-commercial purposes. But there were now challenges to Edison's patents arising in America and Europe, and Edison had become wary of ever again displaying any of his prototypes to the public in so much detail, lest the same thing happen. When Edison canceled a public demonstration of his platinum filament incandescent bulb—which still melted if burned for longer than three minutes—it was because he knew he would not be able to fool a scientifically literate audience the way he had fooled the reporters visiting his lab. But he claimed that he had been advised by his lawyers not to display his lights publicly until they were ready for commercial production, in case of further patent challenges.

By November of 1878, a few newspapers were beginning to suspect that the view inside his laboratory was not as rosy as he was making it out to be. This may have been due to the fact that Edison had been forced to give an unsatisfactory progress report to his investors, who in turn gossiped about it where reporters could hear, or it may have been due to natural skepticism produced by the fact that Edison kept making promises that he had not yet fulfilled. In either case, an editorial in the *Brooklyn Daily Eagle* from that same year and month takes on a suspicious tone not at all in keeping with the normal effusive reporting on Edison that appeared in the New York papers. It reads:

"Professor Edison seems to have some prospect of trouble in getting his electric light before the public as a permanent institution. It is asserted that his divisible electric light is not a new invention, it having been patented more than thirty years ago by a man who died before he could reap any of the benefits of his discovery. And while this delay is retarding the practical application of the light here, the people of the Old World are using an electric light which is equally as valuable as the one Edison proposes to give us. It is in fact the same light under a different name, and in one city at least, that of St. Petersburg, it has proven entirely successfully. If Edison does not hurry up and put his light in use, we shall soon be asking for the Jaklockkoff light, only we will change its name before adopting it."

Unbeknownst to the unnamed author of this article, in late November of 1879, precisely one year after it was written, Edison's experiments on the incandescent light bulb would finally yield significant progress, in the form of a durable, clean-burning filament.

A new filament

Edison and his men were working 12 hour days, from 7 in the evening to 7 in the morning, because the laboratory received so many visitors during the day that it was impossible to get anything accomplished during daylight hours. Shortly after the formation of his Electric Light Company, he had been forced to confess to his investors that he had encountered much greater difficulties in his experiments with platinum filament than he initially led the public to believe. He did not tell them the whole truth, which was that he had never made any breakthroughs with platinum filament at all, but he was at least more forthcoming than he was with reporters. Edison told one journalist that his work was getting along so well that even when he made errors, they ended up improving his lightbulb in some way. But in private, in the company of his laboratory assistants, he finally acknowledged that the platinum filament experiment was a dead end, and that it was time to experiment with other materials.

The problem with carbon filaments—the most promising candidate apart from platinum—was that they burned out too quickly. Edison found a solution to this problem by using, first carbonized sewing thread, then carbonized paper as filaments. These materials did not melt or burn out, but they oxidized quickly, which made the light darker and dimmer. The oxidation problem was solved by creating a vacuum inside the bulb—a painstaking process which many inventors had tried and failed before. In vacuum, the carbonized sewing thread filament burned steadily for well over twenty four hours, only for the bulb to explode when the voltage was increased. At last, the carbonized paper filament was substituted—and this time, the filament was bent into the shape of a horse shoe. It proved even more durable than the thread filament, and overnight, shares in Edison's Electric Light Company went through the roof.

After this breakthrough, Edwin Fox of the New York Herald, one of the reporters Edison had taken into his confidence, spent two weeks at Menlo Park, observing the daily routine of Edison's life and work. A few weeks later, on December 21, 1879, Fox published a long and flattering article entitled "Edison's Light", a portion of which is excerpted below:

"The near approach of the first public exhibition of Edison's long looked for electric light, announced to take place on New Year's Eve at Menlo Park, on which occasion that place will be illuminated with the new light, has revived public interest in the great inventor's work, and throughout the civilized world scientists and people generally are anxiously awaiting the result. From the beginning of his experiments in electric lighting to the present time Mr. Edison has kept his laboratory generally closed, and no authoritative account...of any of the important steps of his program has been made public—a course of procedure the inventor found absolutely necessary for his own protection. The Herald is now, however, enabled to present to its readers a full and accurate account of his work from its inception to its completion.

"Edison's electric light, incredible as it may appear, is produced from a little piece of paper—a tiny strip of paper that a breath would blow away. Through this little strip of paper is passed an electric current, and the result is a bright, beautiful light, like the mellow sunset of an Italian autumn.

"'But paper instantly burns, even under the trifling heat of a tallow candle,' exclaims the skeptic, 'and how, then, can it withstand the fierce heat of an electric current?' Very true, but Edison makes the little piece of paper more infusible than platinum, more durable than granite. And this involves no complicated process. The paper is merely baked in an oven until all its elements have passed away except its carbon framework. The latter is then placed in a glass globe connected with the wires leading to the electricity producing machine, and the air exhausted from the globe. Then the apparatus is ready to give out a light that produces no deleterious gases, no smoke, no offensive odors— a light without flame, without danger, requiring no matches to ignite, giving out but little heat, vitiating no air, and free from all flickering; a light that is a little globe of sunshine, a veritable Aladdin's lamp. And this light, the inventor claims, can be produced cheaper than that from the cheapest oil. Were it not for the phonograph, the quadriplex telegraph, the telephone and the various other remarkable productions of the great inventor the world might well hesitate to accept his assurance that such a beneficent result had been obtained, but, as it is, his past achievements in science are sufficient guarantee that his claims are not without foundation, even though for months past the press of Europe and America has teemed with dissertations and expositions from learned scientists ridiculing Edison and showing that it was impossible for him to achieve that which he has undertaken."

Modern readers must appreciate this eye-witness account from the pages of history: almost anyone living today has taken electric lights for granted for their entire lives. It has therefore probably never occurred to any of us to exclaim over the beauty of the light produced by an incandescent bulb, let alone to compare it to "the mellow sunset of an Italian autumn." Even more difficult for the modern reader to relate to is the sense of wonder that Edison's observers clearly felt at being introduced to a light that would not catch fire if it came in contact with the curtains, or a lady's hair. For all of human history, light had been synonymous with fire, both life-giving and life-threatening. With Edison's invention, light was rendered safe, as if it had been tamed. The electric light may have been less of a bolt from the blue than the phonograph, but it too had introduced something into the sphere of human existence that had never been imagined before.

Although Edison had given Fox access to his laboratory for no other purpose than to write such an article, he was deeply dismayed when it was published. In the first place, any major story appearing the papers about him inevitably produced a new stream of aggravating visitors taking time away from his work. In the second, as the above excerpt demonstrates, Fox effectively did to the electric light what *Scientific American* had done to the phonograph: by revealing the existence of the carbonized cardboard filament and the vacuum chamber in the glass bulb, he had given Edison's competitors the tip they needed to catch up to him.

One of Edison's competitors responded to the article by claiming that Edison must have falsified his results just to raise investment capital for his Electric Light Company. The bulb could not possibly last for longer than three hours, the objection went, and the vacuum chamber in the bulb would burst within a few minutes. Edison responded by announcing that on New Year's Day, he would make a full public demonstration of his electric lights. He had already installed them in his laboratory and his home for visitors to see. Now he proposed to install them in ten more houses in Menlo Park, and in ten street lamps. The general public would be invited to visit and see the lights for themselves. Naturally, such a claim excited a great deal of public interest, but it worried Edison's investors, who understood that if anything were to go wrong with the demonstration it would be highly damaging to Edison's reputation and to his company. They begged him to install the lights two weeks prior to the public's arrival, just to ensure that they would work. Edison came as near to compromising as he ever did by installing the lights a day in advance of the public demonstration.

So many people arrived to take in the electric light spectacle that extra trains were scheduled to run from New York to Menlo Park. Edison's laboratory assistants were unable to do any work—instead, they tried to keep visitors from touching any of the prototypes or equipment, particularly after one man broke a vacuum pump. Edison tried to hide from the crowds, but inevitably, they sought him out, and he was forced into the tedious chore of answering the same questions and providing the same explanations many times over. And this was not even the worst part of overrun by so many strangers—among the curious, idle spectators were corporate spies and saboteurs. Edison's assistants intercepted one person who had smuggled wires under his suit in the act of trying to make the light bulb exhibit short-circuit. He turned out to be an electrician, and he was in the employ of a Maryland gas company that wished to discredit Edison before he could pose serious competition to the gas monopoly. The exhibition ran for only two days before Edison closed the laboratory down again on January 2, 1880.

Chapter Five: Edison in Manhattan

Ships and trains

Shortly after his New Year's exhibition at Menlo Park, Edison was hired to outfit the luxury steamship *Columbia* with electric lights. It would be the first time that Edison's lights had ever been put to use outside the town of Menlo Park or his own laboratory, but Edison was eager to tackle the project. In later years, when Edison Electric had branches all over the world, Edison's lights would be in huge demand on ships, as the public developed an insatiable appetite for the ethereal spectacle of an electrified ship gliding down the water in the darkness, and the Columbia was the ship that started the craze. Electric lights on ships would prove dangerous once they were more common, as the wiring was prone to sparking, and fires at sea are catastrophic, but the lighting of the *Columbia* proved a success for Edison. During the ship's maiden voyage around Cape Horn, however, passengers were forbidden from switching the lights in their cabins on or off; they had to call a steward in the morning and in the evening to open a lockbox near the door and operate the switch for them.

Once again displaying his infinite capacity for allowing new enthusiasms to sidetrack his work on projects that were in development, Edison took time away from producing a commercial version of his electric lights to work on electric trains in 1880. His idea was that an electrified train track, with an asphalt coating to ground it and protect it from water, would be safer and faster than any other train; furthermore, it could be fully automated and controlled by telegraph signal. Since most train accidents occurred due to human error—as when Edison was 16 and failed to stop an oncoming freight car on a collision course with another train—doing away with the need for human engineers seemed like an excellent idea. The electrification of the rails would prevent the train's wheels from ever jumping the track, the next most frequent cause of accidents. And electrification would enable trains to travel at much faster speeds than those powered by coal or steam. Edison went so far as to build an electrical train track half a mile in length in the fields around Menlo Park. He, his visitors, and his laboratory assistants tested the train by riding it themselves, sometimes for forty miles at a time, until at last the train did jump the tracks, throwing some of the passengers into the grassy fields around them.

Competition

Edison's delay in producing a commercial version of the phonograph could not do him serious damage because it was indisputably his invention and no one could challenge his patents. He therefore had the luxury of taking as much time as he wished in bringing the phonograph to commercial production, because there was no danger of anyone beating him to it, amateurs working from the diagram and specifications in *Scientific American* notwithstanding. The electric light was a very different matter. Scientists, inventors, and engineers had been working on the electric light since decades before Edison was even born; there were a number of different ways to approach the problem of how to make a working, durable electric light, and though Edison's approach was the most successful, the secret of his success had been revealed in the *Herald* article about the carbonized cardboard filaments.

The very same reporter who had written the *Herald* article, Edwin Fox, wrote Edison a letter in October of 1880 urging him to bring the electric light into commercial production soon. Through the window of Fox's office, he could see into the laboratories of the new United States

Electric Light Company, where they were manufacturing bulbs that built on Edison's invention, narrowly skirting patent issues by bending the cardboard filament into an M shape, in tribute to its designer Hiram Maxim (Edison's were bent into the shape of horse shoes.)

In point of fact, new electric light companies were springing up all over New York, and most of them were beating Edison to the punch. Edison had plans to electrify all of lower Manhattan, but in the meantime he was investigating bamboo as a new material for filaments, sending his employees on expeditions to every bamboo-growing country on earth to gather samples so Edison could determine which was the best varietal (he ended up settling on Japanese bamboo.) There were undoubted advantages to the bamboo filament, but it didn't change the fact that while Edison was still refining his electric lights, United States Electric had already opened an office in Manhattan with a reading room lit by one hundred and fifty electric bulbs. Edison expected to waltz effortlessly into a contract with the city to electrify Manhattan, but he was losing ground daily to his competitors. Brush Electric Light Company had already volunteered to light Broadway at no charge to the city, just for the marketing advantage of being the first electric light company on the ground.

Edison had always anticipated that most of his clients would be private business owners—there were still no incandescent light bulbs that were effective for outdoor use, so street lighting was invariably arc lighting, which was not the technology Edison had built his brand around. Now he saw that if he did not pursue public works contracts for street lighting, he would be surrendering a considerable advantage to his competitors. Furthermore, Edison was already having a difficult time negotiating with the city for the right to lay the wiring grid that would be necessary before he could supply electric lighting to commercial customers. In a bid to negotiate reasonable terms for a wiring grid project, Edison put on an enormous light display at Menlo Park once again, this time a private event staged for the benefit of the New York City aldermen who had the final say over the terms of Edison's contract with the city. The lights display was followed by a lavishly catered dinner with lots of champagne. The aldermen returned to the city in an excellent mood, but when negotiations resumed in the days after, Edison balked at the terms they offered. They wanted him to pay ten cents per every foot of wire laid, which, considering the amount of wire necessary to electrify the city, would have cost Edison upwards of a thousand dollars per mile. Eventually they reached terms of five cents per foot.

Leaving Menlo Park

Edison's laboratory at Menlo Park was his ideal working environment for many reasons. He had spent years building it into an isolated paradise for eccentric genius inventors. It was near enough to New York to be convenient but far enough away that he was not nearly as overrun by curious passers-by as he would otherwise have been. He valued autonomy in his working life above all other things, and at Menlo Park he had it. However, in early 1881, his lawyer advised him urgently to consider moving his entire base of operations, as well as himself and his family, to Manhattan. The company could purchase a building to house its offices, which it could completely electrify, which would serve as the best possible advertisement to New Yorkers regarding what Edison's lights could do. Edison himself would have to be on hand for the effect to be complete, which would necessitate his living in the city. Edison knew that this would move would require him to interact with even more idle visitors than he had been troubled by at Menlo Park, and that he would have to devote even more of his time to giving demonstrations and answering repetitive questions. But he came to be convinced that doing so would be in the best interests of the company, and therefore the Fifth Avenue offices of Edison's Electric Light Company became his new base of operations.

Edison next had to purchase land in Manhattan to house the dynamo he would need to build in order to power the electric lights he was trying to sell. Even in 1881, Manhattan was prohibitively expensive, and even purchasing the most dilapidated buildings he could find, in the worst area of town he knew of, he had to spend one hundred and fifty times the amount of money he anticipated spending. On top of that, he had to form an entirely new company to construct the dynamo, because the investors of Edison Electric did not wish to expand their interests in that direction; Edison formed the Edison Machine Works Company as a result.

The dangers of electricity

Edison was informed by the city of New York that his workmen would be subject to the oversight of five safety inspectors, whose job was to ensure that the electric wiring was being laid in safely. Edison would be responsible for paying the inspectors himself. He did not mind the expense so much as he worried that the work would be delayed by the inspector's safety concerns—but as it turned out, he had nothing to worry about. The safety inspectors only ever appeared briefly for a few minutes on paydays, and otherwise left Edison's workmen alone.

But safety around electricity was, in general, starting to become a matter of general concern. Nowadays, everyone is taught from the time they are young children to be cautious of electricity, not to touch exposed wiring, not to stick fingers or metal objects into wall outlets. But there was no such universal understanding of how electricity worked in 1881, and though electrical engineers were well aware of the need for caution, uninitiated strangers visiting labs and factories for the first time were not, and the electricians did not always think to warn them. As electric wiring became more commonplace, deaths from electrical accidents naturally increased in number.

Edison Electric had as yet seen no fatal accidents amongst its workers or visitors, but some of their competitors had, and Edison hastened to assure the public that he worked only with direct current electricity, unlike the companies responsible for the deaths, who worked with alternating current. This was the first feint in what would later come to be known as "the War of the Currents", a prolonged and strangely vicious publicity battle that would pit Edison against his most famous historical rival, Nikola Tesla.

Edison biographer Randall Stross provides this useful explanation clarifying the difference between direct current and alternating current:

"Direct current flows in the same direction; alternating current flows in one direction, then reverses and flows in the other, continuously changing. Both forms of current could electrically shock a human being, causing sustained contraction of muscles. Alternating current poses an especially dangerous risk, however, because its rapid discontinuous movement—flowing in this direction, then that one—is more likely to scramble the neural subsystem that serves as the heart's guiding metronome. Once the signals are scrambled, fibrillation follows: rapid, ineffective contractions of the heart muscles that fails to pump blood as it should. Alternating current's propensity to induce fibrillation gives direct current an edge in terms of safety."

A common sight in large American cities during electricity's early years involved horses behaving strangely in the vicinity of electric wiring—bolting, rearing, taking off suddenly at a gallop, to the consternation of their drivers. It also sometimes happened that men and women walking down the street found their feet, or their whole bodies, prickling unpleasantly. This was the result of electricity "leaks", places where the insulation on the wiring was fault, feeding electricity into the earth, which conducted the charge weakly. Edison first began experiencing problems of this nature at his Pearl Street station, but he was not forthcoming with the public about them, even—or perhaps especially—after newspaper reporters descended on his offices, demanding statements and explanations. Edison's people went so far as to proclaim that not only had no accident occurred, an accident of that nature was not even possible. The truth was precisely the opposite, as Edison knew all too well.

Electricity versus gas

Before the War of the Currents, there was the war between electrical companies and gas companies. As we discussed in a previous chapter, the gas industry was a powerful monopoly in the 1880's, and once it began to perceive Edison and other electric light providers as a direct threat to its business, it did not hesitate to use unscrupulous means to try to persuade the public that if they changed their homes over from gas to electricity, they were courting death. This was the same industry that sent a saboteur to Edison's laboratory with instructions to short-circuit his incandescent bulbs during a demonstration, but even that was a fairly innocent gesture in comparison to the lengths they were prepared to go to preserve their monopoly.

Edison and the other electrical companies responded by enthusiastically calling attention to every gas explosion that occurred, every suspicious death that might be attributable to gas poisoning. They produced reams of literature on the subject, including pamphlets that compared the oxygen content of a room with a single person reading by gaslight to be similar to the oxygen content of a room without gas, containing 23 people. It was incontrovertible that gas had a distinctive odor, stained the walls and furnishing, and emitted fumes, and that, by contrast, electric light was odorless, tasteless, and did not emit heat. But comparing the inconveniences of gas to the conveniences of electricity was not enough; the electrical companies wished to fix it prominently in the public's mind that to use gas power in their homes was to court death. And the gas companies' propaganda claimed precisely the same thing about the electrical companies. The claims made by both sides were specious at best, outright falsehood at worst, but the gas companies' goal was to maintain control of the largest utility in the country—the amount of money involved made people ruthless.

By contrast, the electrical companies' goal was to sell a new product, and in a larger sense, a new idea, to the American people. The fact that the properties of electricity were still deeply mysterious to the public allowed the gas companies to hint at all sorts of deathly consequences for using it, but at the same time, it allowed the electrical companies to make any number of miraculous, bizarre, and whimsical claims about its beneficial properties. Readers of newspapers became accustomed to hearing electricity being credited for literally all manner of improvements to physical health, mental health, and appearance.

The following article, "A New Use of Electricity", appeared in the *New York Times* on January 12, 1882. It is an excellent example of tongue-in-cheek contemporary reactions to the various consumer goods that flooded the market after having been electrified in one way or another, and to the over the top claims made by advertisers on behalf of those products:

"The uses of electricity are growing every day, especially the uses made of it by ingenious advertisers. The electric hair-brush, which is warranted to make hair grow on the head of a brass monkey if it used sufficiently often, has been before the public for some time, and until lately was justly regarded as furnishing the easiest and most effectual way of applying electricity to the skin. It is now, however, rivaled in the estimation of the public by the electric corset, a new and wonderful invention. The wood-cut showing the manner of using the electric corset represents that article as a sort of close-fitting jacket worn by a young lady, the sleeves and neck of whose dress are really a little too—shall we say alarming? The wood-cut is necessary, for although the advertisers informs the public that the electric corset is precisely like the ordinary corset in appearance, his words convey no idea to any upright and honorable man. If steadily worn, this electric corset will cause the wearer to grow plump and to enjoy the very best of health—that is, if we may believe what the advertiser says. As it is asserted to be perfectly harmless, and to convey no perceptible shock to the human arm, it ought to become at least as popular as the electric hair-brush has been. Nevertheless, in spite of the merits of the electric corset, a new discovery has lately been made in regard to the electric hair brush which, when it becomes generally known, will make the latter altogether the most desirable object that a woman can possibly have in the house.

"Like many other great discoveries, the one in question was made by accident. It has long been a matter of tradition that the maternal slipper is the instrument with which nursery discipline is enforce. This was undoubtedly true many years ago when slippers were universally worn, and many of the holiest recollections of the childhood of men of the present generation are associated with the slippers of their mothers. But the old-fashioned slipper, which could be slipped from the foot and applied where it would do the most good at a moment's notice, has, to a great extent, passed away. The buttoned boot has succeeded it, and not only is it impossible for an earnest mother with a large family to unbutton and button up again her boot a dozen times in a day, but the boot itself is too heavy and coarse an instrument to be used in inculcating oral lessons. Hence it is that the hair-brush has become a popular means of training children in the right way. It is always within easy reach; it has a convenient handle, and the back of it, being broad and nearly flat, will cover more surface at a blow than could be covered by any ordinary boot or slipper. Now and then a badly made hairbrush is broken when brought in contact with a particularly bad boy, but as a rule it is a remarkably effective remedial agent.

"Mrs. McFarren, of Bristol, R.I., has a small boy, now of the 6 years, who has given her much anxiety[...] A year ago Mrs. McFarren was prevailed upon to buy an electric hair-brush, with the view of improving the condition of her hair. As the brush was an unusually large and strong one, she naturally used it in the education of her boy. The first time that it was applied to him he had been guilty of some particularly heinous juvenile crime, and was therefore punished with more than usual severity. To his mother's surprise, the moment he was released he sprang up and turned several hand-springs, at the same time breaking forth into song. For the rest of the day he was in the very highest spirits, and not a trace of his former sullen manner was visible. This was such an unexpected and utterly unprecedented state of things that his mother could account for it only on the supposition that the effects of four years of frequent punishment had been cumulative, and had only just begun to show itself.

"The boy continued to get into mischief and was, of course, daily punished. Every time that the hair-brush was applied to him his spirits seemed to rise and his muscular activity increased. Moreover, he suddenly began to grow tall and strong, and his various bodily ailments disappeared. At the end of a year, he was the tallest, heaviest, and strongest boy of his age in the whole town, and although his restless activity constantly led him into breaches of maternal law, nothing could check the flow of his spirits or spoil his perennial good humor.

"There can be no reasonable doubt that these wonderful changes in the mental and physical constitution of the McFarren small-boy were due to the electrical properties of the hair-brush used by his mother during the past year. The electricity, driven into his system by impact, filled him with high spirits and gave an imulse to his physical growth. It is thus evident that the ability of the electrical hair-brush to infuse electricity into the scalp and thus promote the growth of the hair is its least valuable property. Hereafter it will be used not merely as the universal instrument of juvenile punishment, but as the readiest and surest means of infusing vitality into the sick and weakly of whatever age, and Mrs. McFarren's name will be forever associated with the greatest of the electrical discoveries."

The craze for electrified household objects continued for several years, and the gas companies were not ultimately successful in persuading the public to shun electricity as dangerous. Edison Electric received between three and four thousand applications from private customers to install electric lighting in prisons, factories, and hotels in from 1881 to 1882, most of which the company was obliged to turn down. Any customer seeking electrical power at their facility, unless they lived on one of the streets where Edison's men were already laying down the power grid, would have to also build their own generator plants, a project that was a great deal more expensive and troublesome for Edison's company than it was profitable.

Success at Pearl Street Station

Though he could have made a considerable amount of money off the thousands of customers who were interested in contracting with Edison Electric to build their own on-site power plants,

Edison viewed such projects as a distraction from his main priority. His eye was fixed on a future in which every American city would be completely on the power grid, and any customer who wanted electrical power could obtain it simply by tapping into an existing system. Building grids in cities across the country was the key to making electrical power a permanent and necessary aspect of American life. (Edison was rather more willing to build generators and lay in electricity for customers in foreign countries, where he did not need to invest so heavily in the infrastructure.) The first step towards this goal was, of course, to electrify Manhattan, but it was taking longer than anticipated to finish the first portion of the grid. As delays mounted, stock in gas companies began to rise again, a sign that the public's faith in Edison had begun to falter. His reputation took a further blow when he installed a generator plant at the home of billionaire William Vanderbilt, only to be forced to remove it on the orders of Vanderbilt's wife, when the new electrical wiring caused the metallic wallpaper in the drawing room to begin to smolder.

Undeterred by the disaster at the Vanderbilts' home, fellow billionaire J. Pierpont Morgan, the largest private investor in Edison Electric, had a generator plant built on his grounds, and electric lights (including a kind of portable electric desk lamp that had never been seen before) installed in his home. The prototype desk lamp, which was wired through the desk itself from a metal plate in the floor, caused the entire desk to catch fire when it was first turned on, but unlike Mrs. Vanderbilt, Morgan merely demanded that the system be re-installed in a less ignitable way.

Edison Electric completed work on the underground conductors at Pearl Street on September 4, 1882, inaugurating electric light service for some three thousand customers. The spectacle of indoor lighting came as a disappointment to some—most people's experience with electric lights was confined to the arc lighting that illuminated the streets, and arc lighting was many hundreds of times brighter than the incandescent bulbs Edison used. But when the lights came on at the *New York Times* and the *Herald*, the writers and editors who had spent a lifetime laboring by the light of candles and gas jets praised the superiority of Edison's electrical lights in the warmest possible terms. In general, however, the general public took little notice of this landmark moment in the history of technology: Edison had been promising to light Manhattan since 1878, and four years later, the electric light was no longer a novelty. As Stross puts it, "the moment [was] a satisfying denouement to a long-running drama involving unfulfilled promises and a loud chorus of skeptics."

Edison gave his first batch of customers four months of free service while he devised a meter that could measure the amount of electricity used each month, which was necessary in order to know what to charge. People were happy enough to take advantage of this offer at first, but when electricity began to cost money, there was a general reluctance to switch over from gas, even though Edison promised that electricity would be cheaper. In the end, only 231 customers retained Edison Electric's services after the free trial period ended—a very far cry from the resounding commercial success Edison had anticipated. By the end of the first year, the number of customers had increased to 455, still far below projected numbers.

Edison had let it be known that he intended to open a second power station in a different part of Manhattan immediately after the successful opening of the one at Pearl Street, but this proved impracticable in the short term, as Pearl Street did not begin to turn a profit until it had been in operation for two years (and even then, not until after Edison recruited an outside manager, promising him a bonus of ten thousand dollars if he could get the station out of the red.) His investors urged him to focus his concentration on the one product he was managing to sell at a clip, the off-site private generator plants. Though still convinced that the future lay in centralized power for all urban areas, he grew resigned to the fact that the distributed power plants were the only Edison product then selling at a steady profit. Edison had always resented having to send his most talented people to distant states and cities to oversee the installation of the distributed generators when he needed them in Manhattan to make the Peal Street project run more smoothly. But with work on the Manhattan grid on a hiatus that would last until 1888, he allowed the distributed generator plants to become the full time job of most of his employees.

Chapter Six: Edison Reborn

Death of Mary Stilwell Edison

Biographies of Thomas Edison tend to dwell only lightly on the subject of Mary Edison. Due to her own self-effacing personality and Edison's habit of neglecting, or at least ignoring, home and family life to focus on his inventions, she simply makes very few appearances in any narrative of Edison's early life. The newspaper reporters who flocked to Edison's side during his Menlo Park days did not always interact with her or the children, and those reporters who did meet her had little to say about her that could not be said about any well-to-do 19th century housewife whose husband they wished to flatter: she was regarded as charming and good looking, a devoted mother, and a perfect match to Edison. Journalists who wrote of her at all tended to cast her as the comic stock character of the bemused wife whose absent-minded husband drives her to fond distraction. Such a portrayal of Edison undoubtedly has some basis in reality. He was notoriously distractible, and he once appeared for Sunday dinner in a brand new, highly expensive wool suit his wife had purchased for him, only to leave the table and plunge into a week of nonstop work, during which he never changed clothes—the suit was obviously ruined. But no real remembrance of Mary Edison survives, except in these unrevealing caricatures. Edison rarely spoke of her, or even made reference to her in his diaries, unless it was to criticize her intelligence.

Shortly after they were married, Edison had taken Mary on as an assistant in his laboratory, only to abruptly change his mind and send her back home when she had been working with him only a few days. "Dearly beloved wife cannot invent worth a damn," he wrote in his diary at the time—a fact which is scarcely to be wondered at, considering that she was only sixteen years old at the time of their marriage, and unlike Edison, had not been messing around with chemicals and conducting independent science experiments in train cars from the age of twelve onwards. Some years later, Edison was speaking to a colleague who was about to become engaged. When Edison was shown a photograph of the man's prospective bride, he absently praised her looks, then remarked suddenly, "Why is it...that so few women have *brains?* Men of brains it is easy to find, but *women—*"

Edison and Mary must have been on sufficiently good terms with each other to produce their three children, but one cannot help but wonder whether his continuous absences from home were due entirely to his obsessive work ethic, or whether he did not feel himself disappointed, justly or unjustly, by the wife he had chosen for himself. If he was disappointed, he seems at least not to have reproached her for it. Considering that he was nine years Mary Edison's senior, and barely knew her at all when he made up his mind to marry her, he probably realized it would have been unfair of him to do so.

For several years prior to her death, Mary Edison had been experiencing health problems. The precise nature of her illness is difficult to determine. While Edison was on his trip to Wyoming and California, during his wife's third pregnancy, he received a letter from one of his assistants informing him that Mrs. Edison was very unwell:

> "Mrs. E's health is not of the best—She is extremely nervous and frets a great deal about you, and about everything—I take it to be nervous prostration—She was so frightened yesterday for fear the children would get on the track that she fainted—This morning I telegraphed Dr. Ward who came at noon…She needs a change and right away, as the cars can

keep her awake at night and this causes her to lose strength."

"Nervous prostration" was a highly nonspecific diagnosis in 19th century medicine. It covered a wide range of symptoms stemming from a vast number of unidentified complaints. Women were thought to be especially prone to it, as the condition was thought to be synonymous with anxiety and emotional distress, a reflection of female fragility. The treatments generally recommended for this affliction were rest, change of scenery, and "nerve tonics", which included drugs like laudanum and morphine. There are no surviving details as to what treatments Mary Edison received for her illnesses, but her health remained in a fragile state for the last several years of her life. Edison seems not to have believe that she was in much danger—he declined to cut his trip west short when he received word of Mary's illness, even though she was pregnant at the time. But she was certainly incapacitated. By the time of her death, her mother had already been the full-time caretaker of the Edison children for awhile, a job she would probably not have been called upon to do if Mary Edison were in good enough condition to care for them herself.

After Edison finished building the power grid at Pearl Street, he decided to retire from the inventing side of Edison Electric and devote himself entirely to the more mundane work of business for about a year. Once there was no need for Edison to be physically present in Manhattan all the time, Mary Edison insisted that they move back to their home at Menlo Park. In the spring of 1881 she wrote to a friend, "I am so awfully sick I am afraid… My head is nearly splitting and my throat is very sore." The Edison family returned to Menlo Park in the early summer; a couple of months later, on August 9, 1881, Mary Stilwell Edison died. She was only twenty nine years old.

The circumstances of Mary Edison's death are something of a mystery, medically speaking. The official cause of death was listed as "congestion of the brain", a condition which, like "nervous prostration", has no precise meaning in modern medical science. However, new research into Thomas Edison's papers, a project run by Rutgers University, suggests that Mary Edison's health problems had been treated with morphine over the course of several years, and that morphine played a role in her death. In the 19th century, morphine was readily available without a prescription, and doctors dispensed it liberally to young women afflicted with "nervous complaints".

One newspaper—one of the few to have ever published a personal interview with Mary Edison—claimed, after her death, that she had been a long time user of morphine, and that she had in fact died of a morphine overdose, though there is no indication whether the overdose was taken intentionally or accidentally, or whether it was self-administered or administered by a doctor. It also claimed that moments after Mary Edison's death, her husband attempted to revive her by administering electrical shocks. Research reveals that "congestion of the brain", her cause of death, was then considered a visible symptom of death by morphine overdose, and that electrical shocks were sometimes recommended to "revive" the patient.

Whatever the cause of Mary Edison's death, it had a profound impact on Thomas Edison—rather more profound, perhaps, than anyone would have guessed, knowing how distant their relationship had been. He seemed to be overcome by guilty feelings, as if it suddenly seemed to him that he had neglected his wife during her long illness—perhaps he had never believed that anything was seriously wrong with her, only to find himself proven terribly wrong.

His daughter Marion, nicknamed Dot, later recalled that she awoke the next morning to find her father "shaking with grief, weeping and sobbing so he could hardly tell me that Mother had died in the night." Marion Edison was twelve years old at the time; her brother Tom was eight, and her brother Will was five. His wife's death seemed to suddenly awaken Edison to the fact that he had children. He had never been involved in their lives, and had sometimes gone so long without seeing them that they grew unrecognizable to him in the gaps between visits, but that was to change—at least, where Marion was concerned. Tom and Will, who were educated at boarding schools, were not to see much of their father in the coming years, but Marion became his principle companion for a time. He withdrew her from Madam Mears's French Academy on Madison Avenue and brought her home to live with him; he bought her a horse and a parrot and took her into the laboratory with him to work as his assistant. (As a joke, and perhaps to help her blend into an otherwise all male environment, Edison came up with a new nickname for her during her laboratory hours: George.) He also took over her education, in a rather eccentric fashion: her lessons consisted solely of reading ten pages out of the encyclopedia daily. They took carriage drives through the country, with Marion holding the reins of the horse, as Edison was a bad driver. Marion Edison was to remain at her father's side for the next few years, until he remarried; as a teenager, she would return to boarding school.

Summer of 1885: Mina Miller and the Chautauqua Institute

After his wife's death, and once the electric light was ensconced in the commercial realm and no longer needed his personal oversight, Edison began to feel that he was at loose ends. He decided to take a formal break from work, the first time he had done so since he was twelve years old.

During the summer of 1885, a year after Mary Edison's death, Edison took a vacation to the Chautauqua Institution at Chautauqua Lake, New York, a kind of retreat center for recreational learning—like a modern day summer camp with educational lectures, but for adults as well as children. He had been invited to attend a session at the Institute and give lectures a few years earlier, but had balked at the last minute and traveled west instead. Now, however, he had an interest in the institute he did not have before: one of the institute's two founders, Lewis Miller, had a nineteen year old daughter named Mina, whom Edison wanted to marry. Edison and Mina were introduced by the wife of one of Edison's business partners; he had asked her to introduce him to any eligible young ladies she thought he might get along with. After she arranged for Edison to meet Mina Miller at a world's fair exhibition in New Orleans (where Edison Electric had won a contract to illuminate the main building) Edison was invited to make the visit to the Chautauqua Institute that he had postponed a few years before. As Mina was going as well, it was an invitation he accepted, and he brought his daughter Marion along with him.

One of the activities at this proto-summer camp involved all the guests keeping a personal diary for 10 straight days. Edison was a habitual keeper of diaries, but they had always been technical in nature, containing sketches and diagrams related to his inventions, with only passing comments related to his personal life. But the diary he produced at the Chautauqua Institute is of a very different character: it is full of wry humor and observations about his activities, the books he was reading, and the people he spent the most time with, including his daughter and Mina Miller.

The diary reveals a side of Thomas Edison otherwise obscured by the flat details of his autobiography. A man so focused on outward action as Edison did not give observers much opportunity to glimpse his inner thoughts and feelings. To read about Edison's life up to the age of 38 is to read about a man continually doing things, building things, thinking of new things to do and build. To read the diary he kept during the summer of 1885 is to glimpse the busy, humorous, tender, creative brain that made all the doing and building possible. His writing style possessed a richness that most people would not suspect of a person so purely devoted to technology and science; but it is easy to tell, reading it, that Edison was a life-long lover of novels and literature, in addition to his other accomplishments. The first day's diary entry appears in excerpt below:

"Menlo Park N.J., Sunday, July 12, 1885

"Awakened at 5:15 a.m. My eyes were embarrassed by the sunbeams. Turned my back to them and tried to take another dip into oblivion. Succeeded. Awakened at 7 a.m. Thought of Mina, Daisy, and Mamma G. Put all 3 in my mental kaleidoscope to obtain a new combination a la Galton. Took Mina as a basis, tried to improve her beauty by discarding and adding certain features borrowed from Daisy and Mamma G. A sort of Raphaelized beauty, got into it too deep, mind flew away and I went to sleep again.

"Awakened at 8:15 a.m. Powerful itching of my head, lots of white dry dandruff. What is this d—mnable material? Perhaps it's the dust from the dry literary matter I've crowded into my noddle lately. It's nomadic, gets all over my coat, must read about it in the Encyclopedia.

"Smoking too much makes me nervous. Must lasso my natural tendency to acquire such habits. Holding heavy cigar constantly in my mouth has deformed my upper lip, it has a sort of Havana curl.

"Arose at 9 o'clock, came down stairs expecting twas too late for breakfast. Twasn't. Couldn't eat much, nerves of stomach too nicotinny. The roots of tobacco plants must go clear through to hell. Satan's principal agent Dyspepsia must have charge of this branch of the vegetable kingdom.

"It has just occurred to me that the brain may digest certain portions of food, say the ethereal part, as well as the stomach. Perhaps dandruff is the excreta of the mind — the quantity of this material being directly proportional to the amount of reading one indulges in. A book on German metaphysics would thus easily ruin a dress suit.

"After breakfast start[ed] reading Hawthorne's English Notebook. Don't think much of it. Perhaps I'm a literary barbarian and am not yet educated up to the point of appreciating fine writing. 90 per cent of his book is descriptive of old churches and graveyards and coroners. He and Geo Selwyn ought to have been appointed perpetual coroners of London. Two fine things in the book were these. Hawthorne shewing to little Rose Hawthorne a big live lobster told her it was a very ugly thing and would bite everybody, whereupon she asked "if the first one God made bit him." Again: "Ghostland is beyond the jurisdiction of veracity."

"I think freckles on the skin are due to some salt of Iron, sunlight brings them out by reducing them from high to low state of oxidation. Perhaps with a powerful magnet applied for some time, and then with proper chemicals, these mudholes of beauty might be removed.

"Dot is very busy cleaning the abode of our deaf and dumb parrot. She has fed it tons of edibles and never got a sound out of it. This bird has the taciturnity of a statue, and the dirt producing capacity of a drove of buffalo.

"This is by far the nicest day of this season, neither too hot [n]or too cold. It blooms on the apex of perfection — an Edenday. Good day for an angels' picnic. They could lunch on the smell of flowers and new mown hay, drink the moisture of the air, and dance to the hum of bees. Fancy the soul of Plato astride of a butterfly, riding around Menlo Park with a lunch basket.

"Nature is bound to smile somehow. Holzer has a little dog which just came on the veranda. The face of this dog was as dismal as a bust of Dante, but the dog wagged its tail continuously. This is evidently the way a dog laughs. I wonder if dogs ever go up to flowers and smell them. I think not. Flowers were never intended for dogs and perhaps only incidentally for man, evidently Darwin has it right. They make themselves pretty to attract the insect world who are the transportation agents of their pollen,   pollen freight via Bee line.

"There is a bumblebees nest somewhere near this veranda, several times one came near me. Some little information (acquired experimentally) I obtained when a small boy causes me to lose all delight in watching the navigation of this armed flower burglar.

"Had dinner at 3 p.m. Ruins of a chicken, rice pudding. I eat too quick.

"At 4 o'clock Dot came around with her horse "Colonel" and took me out riding. Beautiful roads. Saw 10 acre lot full [of] cultivated red raspberries. "A burying ground" so to speak. Got this execrable pun off on Dot. Dot says she is going to write a novel, already started on. She has the judgement of a girl of 16 although only 12. We passed through the town of Metuchen. This town was named after an Indian chief, they called him Metuchen the chief of the rolling lands, the country being undulating. Dot laughed heartily when I told her about a church being a heavenly fire-escape.

"Returned from drive at 5 p.m. Commenced [to] read short sketches of life's Macauley, Sidney Smith, Dickens, and Charlotte Bronte. Macauley when only 4 years old [was an] omnivorous reader, used book language in his childish conversations. When 5 years old, [a] lady spilled some hot coffee on his legs. After a while she asked him if he was better. He replied "Madam the agony has abated." Macauley's mother must have built his mind several years before his body.

"Don't like Dickens — don't know why. I'll stock my literary cellar with his works later. Charlotte Bronte was like DeQuincy, what a nice married couple they would have been. I must read Jane Eyre.

"Played a little on the piano. It's badly out of tune. Two keys have lost their voice.

"Dot just read to me outlines of her proposed novel, the basis seems to be a marriage under duress. I told her that in case of a marriage to put in bucketfuls of misery. This would make it realistic. Speaking of realism in painting etc, Steele Macaye at a dinner given to H H Porter, Wm Winter and myself told us of a definition of modern realism given by some Frenchman whose name I have forgotten, 'Realism, a dirty long haired painter sitting on the head of a bust of Shakespeare painting a pair of old boots covered with dung.' The bell rings for supper. I go."

The diary is quite funny and entertaining, and it is easy to understand why that should be the case: it was meant for public consumption. Everyone at the institute who participated in the diary-keeping project was to read the other guests' offerings, which meant that Edison's remarks about Mina Miller were made in the knowledge that she would read them, along with his remarks about his daughter's cleverness and his thoughts about marriage generally. She must have been impressed, because she ended up joining the Edisons and another family in New Hampshire for the next leg of their summer vacation. During the carriage trip through the mountains, Edison set about teaching Miller how to communicate using the dashes and dots of Morse code, which provided them with an opportunity to "speak" to one another privately, without the other occupants of the carriage being able to understand what they said to one another.

This was a clever move on Edison's part, since it not only enabled them a degree of intimacy that most courting couples were not permitted, it enabled them to get to know one another in a way they otherwise might have struggled with, due to Edison's deafness. For them, Morse stood in for sign language. When Edison proposed to Miller a few weeks later, he tapped the question out to her in the middle of a drawing room full of people. She tapped out a reply of Y-E-S before becoming flustered and leaving the room in a hurry, much to the confusion of her chaperone.

When Edison met Mina Miller, his career was a standstill. Reporters no longer flocked to his doorstep. He was seen as having failed to deliver on the extravagant promises he had made—the electric light was in use, but it had not replaced gas overnight, as he had claimed that it would. Edison was looking for the next big project that would devour his attention, and drag him back into the grueling work routine he depended on. Unbeknownst to him, he would never truly replicate the feverish period of inspiration that produced the phonograph and the electric light—though both of those inventions would have a profound impact on the next few years of his life.

But his marriage to Mina Miller would reinvigorate his sense of purpose. She was devoted to Edison's work, managing their domestic lives around the demands of his laboratory. Years later, after Nikola Tesla had come to work for Edison, he declared that Edison was so sloppy and absentminded in his habits that he would have got nothing done at all if not for the fact that he had married an extremely intelligent woman who ran his life to best advantage. Insofar as it is possible to judge from the outside, Edison's second marriage was far happier than his first—quite possibly because he was a far better husband to Mina than he had been to Mary.

A new home

After their marriage, Edison left it to Mina to decide whether she wanted to live in Manhattan or New Jersey. Mina decided on New Jersey. Edison was able to purchase a large, luxurious furnished home for a quarter of its true value because it had been seized as restitution in an embezzlement case. Edison and Mina named their new home Glenmont. With his family settled, Edison turned his attention to his personal dream project: creating a private laboratory for himself that matched his Menlo Park laboratory in the privacy and autonomy it afforded him, but reflected his increased wealth and status in its state of the art design and equipment. Edison's goal for the lab was that it be outfitted to "build anything, from a lady's watch to a locomotive." The phrase was widely repeated, and though Edison never built either ladies' watches or locomotives, it stood as a kind of symbol for the breadth of his inventiveness for many years.

His initial plan was to form a new research company around the lab and attract investors to pay for it; but Edison had developed a certain reputation for being difficult, based on his dealings with the board of Edison Electric. They wanted him to stay in the laboratory and out of the business side of things; Edison wanted completed autonomy over his company, even at the risk of not making as much money as he could have if he left matters in the hands of more capable managers. He was beginning to see that he would be happier if he simply left the business end of his company to the actual businessmen, but in the meantime, investors had grown wary of working with him. Edison ended up paying for the laboratory out of his own pockets, making him the sole proprietor.

Edison had a number of different inventions he wanted to begin work on in his new lab, which was located in West Orange, New Jersey, including long-abandoned ideas like the hearing aid, and new ideas like the automatic cotton-picker that he'd imagined while on his honeymoon. He most certainly did not want to return to either the phonograph or electric lights, both of which had long ceased to hold his interest. But circumstances impelled him to take up work on the phonograph again for the first time since 1879.

The principle difficulty with Edison's phonograph—the difficulty which had prevented it from being sold for commercial use—was that the cylinder, or record, which the phonographs played, were made of tinfoil, which could not be removed from the phonograph without damaging it. In other words, the phonographs could only ever play the cylinder with which they were sold, a far cry from Edison's vision of selling the phonographs with thousands of cylinders' worth of music.

The only phonographs Edison had ever released were models intended for traveling exhibits, where it wouldn't matter that only the one recording could be played, since the audience would be different every night. In the years since Edison abandoned the phonograph, however, Alexander Graham Bell, inventor of the telephone, had come up with the graphophone—a machine functionally similar to the phonograph, except that it substituted wax cylinders for foil ones. The wax cylinders could be removed and changed for new ones, making the graphophone the first viable device capable of playing music on demand.

The appearance of the graphophone came as a nasty shock to Edison, who, though he had lost interest in his invention, could not bear the thought of someone else improving it and bringing it before the public before he had done so—he was too competitive and too possessive for that. The American Graphophone Company made overtures towards him, recognizing him as the father of the phonograph, offering him considerable shares in the company if he would permit them to use his name. Edison declined the offer and informed his investors that he had a superior version of the wax cylinder in development. Unfortunately, when he tried to demonstrate his finished model to investors, something went wrong. In the words of Alfred Tate, one of Edison's lab assistants:

"Edison was bewildered. There was no possible way in which he could account for such a result Again and again he tried to get that instrument to talk, and again and again it only hissed at him. The time of our guests was limited. They had apportioned one hour for the demonstration, ample time had the instrument functioned. Mr. Dolan and Mr. Cochrane had to catch a train for their homes in Philadelphia and their time for departure came while Edison was still engaged in a futile effort to reproduce his own voice. Most courteously these gentlemen promised to return to the laboratory when Edison had discovered and corrected the obscure defect in the instrument. They left. But they never came back."

The defect proved to be the result of a last minute substitution one of Edison's lab assistants had made to a part of the machine that did not fit as it should have. The damage had been done, however; Edison was unable to attract more investors to launch a competitive product line of phonographs that would compete with graphophones. He had to go into business with a much smaller company that was releasing graphophones alongside phonographs, and even then, he did not enjoy much success.

The original line of phonographs released by Edison's North American Phonograph Company were of poor quality; they broke down frequently, and the wax cylinders were fragile and prone to cracking. Furthermore, Edison was still determined to market the phonograph as an office tool meant for taking dictation and saving the labor of an amanuensis or typist. But the phonograph was not particularly convenient for this purpose, because few people wished to stand perfectly still in one spot speaking down into the phonograph's tube while they took notes. Edison himself did not even use the phonograph for this purpose. The machine reproduced the sound of the human voice comprehensibly; it reproduced the sound of music far better, but Edison still was not sold on the idea of manufacturing phonographs as primarily entertainment devices.

Samuel Insull

A period of deep discouragement followed Edison's defeat in the race to release the phonograph. Neither it nor his electric light ventures were anywhere near as successful as they had promised to become in the late 1870's. Edison gloomily joked to his secretary and personal assistant, Samuel Insull, that he was considering going back to work to earn his living as a telegraph operator, as he had done in his youth. Instead, he made Insull his business manager, and it was under Insull that Edison General Electric Company—still known to the world today as General Electric—would one day come into being.

Samuel Insull had come to work for Edison from his home in England when he was only twenty one years old. He was remarkably talented, and as notable for his exaggerated self-confidence in business matters as he was for being the only person on Edison's staff who knew him well enough to get away with teasing him. Insull had only emigrated to the United States after Edison promised him the post of his own personal secretary—a position of extraordinary responsible for someone so young—and Edison not only gave him the position, he took Insull into his confidence and relied on him as he relied on no other single employee, except possibly Charles Batchelor, who was closer to his own age and had been with him longer.

The trust and confidence between Insull and Edison was mutual. When Insull was placed in charge of the new Edison Machine Works plant in Schenectady, New York, he was forced to take a cut in pay, on top of having to host elaborate parties for Edison's customers out of his own pocket. He chose not to say anything to Edison about it, assuming that it was an oversight that would be corrected eventually.

When Insull made his first annual report to Edison, he had extremely good news to share: vastly improved sales in all product lines, bills paid on time, correspondence streamlined on professional letterheads. Under his guidance, Edison Machine Works began to see profits in the area of one hundred thousand dollars a year, a vast improvement. Edison must have fully recognized what he owed to Insull's management, because he promptly made him a gift of seventy five thousand dollars worth of shares in the company, and when he learned that

Insull had been footing the bill for entertaining clients, including maintaining a stable of horses for them to hunt with, Edison gave him a substantial pay raise and promised that in the future there would be a separate fund allocated just for entertainment expenses.

Edison was still working at his new laboratory complex in West Orange, New Jersey, and rarely found the time to make personal visits to the Schenectady plant, where in the course of six years the workforce had increased from two hundred men to eight thousand. As Insull himself put it, "We never made a dollar until we got the factory 180 miles away from Mr. Edison." Relations between the West Orange and Schenectady sides of the operation were not always completely smooth—Edison, through his lab, did business with the machine works plant, and as with every enterprise that Edison had sole charge of, the labs were not well managed from a business perspective. Bills went unpaid, and

Edison routinely charged the machine works plant twice for laboratory services what he charged anyone else, which Insull found deeply annoying. But Insull would work with Edison for many years, regardless.

Chapter Seven: Edison At War

The War of the Currents

Edison's electric light company was not as successful as its several competitors, a fact which baffled and infuriated him. The chief problem with selling Edison's lights to customers was the same as always: he could not lay in power grids that would provide power to large urban areas without incurring prohibitive costs. His competitors had found a way around this problem, however, thanks to a former Edison employee by the name of Nikola Tesla.

Tesla was a Croatian inventor who had first come to Edison's attention through Charles Batchelor, who oversaw Edison's telephone exchange in Paris at the time Tesla was working there. Tesla had, in a sudden flash of inspiration, come up with a way to build a safe, durable alternating current induction motor, something which

Edison did not believe was possible. Tesla was a young man, and, as he explained to Batchelor, he was extremely eager to make his way to the United States and explain his brilliant new idea to the great and famous Edison in person. Batchelor was profoundly impressed by Tesla, and he gave him a letter of introduction that would secure him a job in one of Edison's American offices. But he warned Tesla that Edison did not want to hear another word about alternating current—he had met with nothing but failure in his own experiments using AC power, and he was determined to have nothing more to do with it.

Tesla found this to be true when he got to the U.S. and met Edison personally, but he worked amicably with Edison for awhile regardless. Tesla left Edison's company over a misunderstanding about money—Edison had made a joke promising Tesla an enormous lump sum of money if he could fix a problem with one of his dynamos. Tesla devoted a year of his life to fixing the problem, and Edison attempted to reward him with a salary raise and a promotion, but Tesla had lost all patience with him. He chose to leave Edison's employ and go into business for himself, which was how he met George Westinghouse. Unlike Edison, Westinghouse was deeply interested in Tesla's alternating current induction motor.

The secret that made alternating current power easier to disperse over a wide area—unlike Edison's direct current, which was still confined to small grids like the Pearl Street station area—was the transformer, which took the blindingly brilliant arc lights used on the streets for outdoor lighting, and allowed them to be turned up or down in intensity, which meant they could be dimmed low enough to be practical for use indoors. The transformer made the transmission of power far more efficient, and therefore far more economical in the long run.

Edison, by the mid 1880's, was being advised by all his top men that Edison Electric needed to develop its own version of an alternating current system if it wanted to remain competitive in the marketplace. But Edison had an entrenched stubbornness on this point that no one could reason with. In the first place, justly or unjustly, Edison felt personally betrayed by Tesla—it offended him that his own former employee had taken the technology Edison rejected and sold it to Edison's competitor. Secondly, he had proprietary feelings towards the electric light business in general—the idea that the technology was developing in a different direction than it had started with him made Edison want to wrest it back onto its original track. Thirdly, he was absolutely convinced that alternating current electricity was deadly dangerous, in a way that direct current was not.

There was some scientific justification for this belief: as we discussed in a previous chapter, all electricity induces muscle spasms when conducted through the human body, but alternating current electricity can induce fibrillation, which is especially dangerous. And there were undoubtedly a number of accidental deaths in the early days of electricity adoption, as people did not yet fully understand how to take proper precautions in the presence of live wires. But Edison had not taken the time to fully understand Tesla's invention before he dismissed it. Tesla's entire motivation in developing the alternating current induction motor stemmed from his witnessing a demonstration of the direct current Gramme dynamo in his engineering school in Austria. Tesla had seen it sparking dangerously, and he had spent the next several years of his life coming up with a solution to that problem. But Edison was incapable of seeing it as the solution to any sort of problem.

The War of the Currents is the name given to the propaganda war that broke out between Edison's company and the alternating current electric companies, Westinghouse in particular. The gas companies had used sabotage and misinformation to try to turn the public off of electricity, and Edison had responded by playing up all the safety issues associated with gas, the fires, the explosions, the poisonous fumes, the unpleasant odors and colors. Death, he strongly implied, was a serious risk for customers who did not switch from gas to electric.

By the late 1880's, the gas companies were no longer a serious threat to Edison's business—not because they had been soundly vanquished, but because the average customer tended to have overlapping gas and electric fixtures. Electric companies using the alternating current system, however, were a very serious threat, and Edison's propaganda machine responded accordingly. As

Tesla biographer Margaret Cheney puts it, "accidents caused by AC must, if they could not be found, be manufactured, and the public alerted to the hazards. Not only were fortunes at stake in the War of the Currents but also the personal pride of an egocentric genius."

A number of stories began appearing in newspapers detailing the grim, sudden deaths of persons accidentally felled by brushes with electrical wires. The example below was printed in the *New York Times* on January 21, 1887. It is entitled, "Struck Dead In A Second":

"Shortly before 5 o'clock yesterday afternoon, when Vesey-street was in its most crowded condition, flames were seen to be issuing from the basement of No. 49, the three-story brick building occupied as a store by William Wilson & Co., who do business under the name of the Centennial American Tea

Company, and who are known to carry a large stock of tea and coffee. As it was only on Wednesday that the neighbors had noticed an unusually large consignment of tea being delivered at No. 49, some interest was felt in the issue of the fire. Before the alarm was responded to the flames had gained considerable ground, and the heat in the narrow street was intense. The passage of the Sixth and Eighth avenue street cars through the thoroughfare was stopped, and Vesey-street was given over to the firemen.

"There was a big cumbersome awning in front of the store and it was found that the wires of the United States Illuminating Company running along above the awning would interfere very considerably with the efforts of the firemen. Superintendent Fred Simmons, of the United States Illuminating Company, was seen at the corner of the street. He was called and assigned to the task of cutting the wires. He was a young, athletic-looking fellow of about 34 years of age, but the work seemed to be so easy and free from danger that the bystanders at first were not particularly interested in his proceedings. He planted his ladder firmly on the ground and ran nimbly up the runs, stopping when his shoulders were about on a level with the wires. He had a pair of pliers in one hand. Slipping one arm through the run of the ladder, he leaned slightly forward and with his other hand cut the wire apart.

"As he did so an arc of light burst forth for one instant and died away. The body of the man quivered in its elevated position, and then doubled itself completely up. A cry went up from the bystanders, who seemed to see at once that the Superintendent had received the full current of the electric fluid coursing through the wires. For a few seconds nothing was done. Then one of the firemen, recovering his presence of mind, jumped upon the shed, moved the wires which the Superintendent still held, and the body fell heavily to the ground, the sound of the head as it struck the pavement being distinctly audible to the spectators.

'"...The clothing of Mr. Simmons was unburned, his features were not in the least distorted, and death might have resulted from heart disease, so free was the appearance of the body from any sign indicative of a painful decease[...] The ambulance surgeon alighted and looked at the body.

'"Why, he'd dead,' he said. 'This isn't a case for the Chambers-street Hospital.'

'"What did he die from?' asked a bystander.

"'This isn't our case,' said the surgeon tersely, and then he hurried away."

In this story, and all like it that appeared throughout the 1880's, there is palpable sense of fear and wonder related to the fact that electricity seemed to be able to kill without leaving any outwardly visible symptom of having passed through the body. Edison found this frustrating. What people could not see, they could not fear as easily as if there were obvious wounds and burns. And it was essential to Edison that people fear alternating current—so essential that he was soon to make the name of alternating current, and its chief advocate George Westinghouse, synonymous with death.

The electric chair

Two days after the above article about the death of Superintendent Simmons of the United States Illuminating Company appeared in the *New*

York Times, an even more ominous article was printed entitled, "To Abolish Hanging: The commission will report in favor of electricity." It reads:

"The report of the Capital Punishment Commission will be presented to the Legislature on Tuesday next. Mr. Elbridge T. Gerry, who has been in Europe for some time, cabled his coadjutors that in case he could not return in time to confer with them, they should make a preliminary report and ask for further time. Dr. Southwick, of this city, another member of the commission, left for Albany yesterday to meet Mr. Matthew Hale, the third member. Before his departure Dr. Southwick was asked what the result of the commission's labors would be. He replied:

'"The weight of opinions expressed in the replies received by the commission in the circular sent out to prominent lawyers, Judges, and others in the State, asking their views on the subject, is against hanging and in favor of electricity. The report, therefore, will be in favor of the adoption of some electrical apparatus for executions. That is the end toward which I have been working for six years, and if the report of our commission does not culminate in the passage of a bill abolishing hanging I shall begin to think that I have been working in vain. I have noticed that the bill introduced in our Legislature last year was copied in Paris, and a similar one has been introduced by a Frenchman in the legislative body of France. Germany has taken up the question, and I have just read that in New Jersey attention has been called to our agitation of the matter. I wish that the Empire State would take the initiative in this step toward a broad humanity. The only argument that can be brought in favor of hanging is that of its deterrent effect, but I maintain that a painless death would have just the same influence upon society if it were accomplished in secret. Let a prisoner be confined in a State prison and be removed from life painlessly and secretly, without the hurrah and sensation that attends a hanging."

The idea that the electric chair was introduced because it was thought to be a painless form of execution may well come as a surprise to modern readers, who are probably familiar with some of the horror stories that come from the execution chamber. Electrocution—a combination of "electrify" and "execute"—as it is practiced by prisons carrying out capital sentences on prisoners, does not in any way resemble Superintendent Simmons' instant, unblemished death. Prisoners executed in the electric chair are essentially cooked to death—their bodies catch fire, their blood boils, their skin falls from their bones. It is not always an instantaneous death. But it is fair to say that when Edison was approached for his help in figuring out a way to execute prisoners by electrical current, he tried his best to make it painless.

And he also did everything he could to make the electric chair serve his own propaganda purposes. When the commission wrote to Edison for his advice, he recommended they use the alternating current dynamo being produced by George Westinghouse. His associates even went so far as to suggest that the name Westinghouse should be used as the verb associated with the action of the machine—in other words, rather than saying prisoners had been electrocuted, one would say they had been "westinghoused". What better way to establish firmly in the minds of the public that alternating current electricity was dangerous than to forever associate it with executions?

The name did not catch on, but the method was set to be tested during the execution of William

Kemmler of Buffalo, New York. Kemmler's attorney objected, naturally, that the state's proposing to use an untested and untried method of execution was a violation of his client's rights—who knew for certain that it would be as painless as Edison claimed? The judge who heard Kemmler's appeal deposed a number of expert witnesses, including Edison, who spoke authoritatively about the amount of electricity needed to kill an adult man. Unbeknownst to the judge, Edison was not yet sure of his facts. For some weeks, he had been experimenting with the voltages needed to execute animals by electricity. As historian Margaret Cheney puts it, "Edison was paying schoolboys twenty-five cents a head for dogs and cats, which he then electrocuted in deliberately crude experiments with alternating current. At the same time he issued scare leaflets with the word 'WARNING!' in red letters at the top." The deaths of these animals served the double purpose of research into electrocution and propaganda against Westinghouse—never mind that direct current was just as capable of taking lives, the fact that alternating current had taken *these* lives was proof that it should be considered too dangerous to be allowed in homes.

Westinghouse was tired of seeing himself and his company run down in the press. Edison's remarks were starting to cross the line from professional insults to personal ones, which Westinghouse found hurtful, particularly since he had made friendly personal overtures to Edison and been rebuffed. According to Edison biographer Randall Stross, Westinghouse published an article in the *North American Review* answering some of Edison's more damaging claims about alternating current:

"Westinghouse also dredged up an old interview with Edison and found this quotation: 'I don't care so much for a fortune as I do for getting ahead of the other fellows.' Westinghouse suggested to readers that it was this, not the supposed merits of Edison's own system, that drove Edison to exaggerate the dangers inherent in the systems of others and to minimize them in his own."

General Electric

In the opinions of most historians, the American consumer was not especially bothered by the War of the Currents—they did not have strong opinions as to whether direct current electricity was safer than alternating current. They preferred alternating current five to one over Edison's direct current simply because it was cheaper and more readily available. Once it became apparent to him that he was losing the War of the Currents, Edison began to withdraw from his own company. Edison General Electric united Edison Electric with Edison Machine Works and all the other smaller companies that existed solely to provide Edison Electric with the parts it needed for manufacturing. Edison sold ninety percent of his stake in the company, netting him about three and a half million dollars cash.

Samuel Insull, Edison's faithful right hand man, was named vice president, and in 1892 he oversaw a merger between Edison General Electric and another electric company, Thomson-Houston; he resigned from the company shortly afterwards. The new company, General Electric, was the first not to bear Edison's name. It is not certain whether this was Edison's choice or not; one version of the story says that Edison refused to permit his name to be associated with it. But his children were wont to say that later in life it was a source of keen disappointment to Edison, that his name had been stripped from the company he had worked to create.

Mining

Ogden, New Jersey, was the site of an iron ore mine which Edison purchased in 1889, a couple of years before walking away from his electric company. Edison had first conceived an interest in mining back during his trip to Wyoming and California, but he had never had the leisure or the resources to fully investigate his ideas; once he had liquidated his shares in General Electric, however, he had the money and the leisure to do anything he wanted. What he wanted above all else, it seems, was the chance of exploring something completely new to him; his favorite part of the inventing process had always been the first year, when ideas flowed rapidly and great leaps could be made overnight. New inventions had a power over his imagination that the mundane business of making a machine cheap enough for commercial sale never did.

Edison spent five years on the mine, and he lived at the Ogden campsite for six out of seven days of the week or longer. Conditions at the camp were harsh; he and his assistants lived in a bare clapboard house (nicknamed the "White House") with no amenities and little protection from the elements. His enthusiasm for the mining project must have been high to keep him there under such conditions, as his marriage to Mina Miller was still relatively new, and their affection was very steady. He wrote a large number of letters to Mina while he was at the mine, and they reveal a side of his personality that is found nowhere else in his personal papers, unless it is hinted at in the diary he kept at the Chautauqua Institute, at the beginning of his and Mina's courtship. In these letters, he addresses Mina as "Billie"—his propensity for giving nicknames to his female relatives continued unabated.

"August 9, 1895: Darling Darling Billy Edison & 2 angels besides. Today has been hotter than the seventh section of hades reserved for Methodist ministers. The humidity was so thick that some of the fish from Hopewell pound swam out into the air. The dust in the mill was frightful—it drove people out of the White House. The cows all left us but we had a banner day... Tomorrow is Saturday and I feel lost I'm not going home to see my darling dustless Billy. What am I to do without a bath, some smartweed seeds have commenced to sprout out of the seams of my coat. Mallory is going to send for a package of flower seeds to plant my clothing. Think of it, Billy darling, your lover turned into a flower garden. I shall feel very lonesome up here Sunday. Would give almost anything to have you and the children here—have written 2 letters previous to this. I hope you will get a good rest and be happy. With each dust mote today as a counter for a kiss I am your lover unchangeable except stranger."

"August 11, 1895: Darling Billie E—It has been warm for the last two days, you went away just in time. It's now raining very hard. I am feeling well and if I were not so very busy I should feel very lonesome. Do you find any little boy out here that compares with Charles? I think you will go a long ways before you find one… Last night I felt blue without you. With a kiss like the swish of a 12 inch cannon projectile I remain, as always, your lover."

"August 12, 1895: Darling Sweetest Loveliest Cutest Extra Billie Edison […] you are the sweetest thing on earth and why should you ever get the <u>blues.</u> You have no earthly reason to get the blues except perhaps disappointment in having such a lover as myself…"

"August 15, 1895: Please Billy darling, don't get so despondent about yourself. There isn't 1 woman in 20000 who is really as smart as yourself. Their apparent smartness is entirely superficial on account of their gift of gab—their judgment isn't worth a cent, your lack of self confidence is the trouble. Getting blue over such things is rotten nonsense. Read the newspapers daring Billy and stop novels. Have all the fun you can. Everything is lovely—and you've got a lover who loves you more and more as we go along. You never need to worry for an instant of his constancy and reliability. So kiss the darlings 21 times each for me and with the usual unlimited amount for yourself."

The iron ore mine was not a success, but Edison enjoyed the work that went into it immensely. When he saw in the newspaper that shares in General Electric were trading at an all time high, he asked a friend to compute how much his own shares would have been worth if he had held onto them; the friend produced the figure of four million dollars. Reportedly, Edison looked very sober for a moment; then his face lit up, and he declared, "Well, we had fun spending it." He had spent it principally on the mine, so his enjoyment of the work must have been profound. Still, though the value of the mine's iron ore proved far lower than original estimates indicated, the project was not a total loss; the equipment Edison invented to process the ore in his new way proved useful in the new industry of manufacturing cement.

Columbia Exposition

With the phonograph, Edison had introduced the world to the possibility of recorded sound. By the time of the 1892 Chicago World's Fair, he was making the first forays into motion pictures, recorded and synchronized with sound. The World's Fair, also called the Columbia Exposition, was held in honor of the five hundredth anniversary of Christopher Columbus discovering the New World. It was meant to showcase everything that was best about America—especially in the fields of invention and technological innovation. There was one entire building at the exposition dedicated exclusively to the wonders of electric lights, and the so-called White City (a temporary village of buildings with whitewashed facades) gleamed brilliantly in the outdoor arc lighting that ran up and down the avenues and canals.

When newspaper reporters asked Edison if he would be bringing anything special to the exposition, he fell back on his old habits with the press, alluding to and describing an invention that did not yet, properly speaking, exist: "My intention is to have such a happy combination of photography and electricity that a man can sit in his own parlor and see depicted upon a curtain the forms of the players in opera upon a distance stage hear the voices of the singers." He was referring to the kinetoscope, the machine which did "for the Eye what the phonograph does for the Ear"—only it could not, yet, do nearly as much as Edison claimed. Furthermore, all that it could do was largely to the credit of his assistant and chief photographer, William Kennedy Laurie Dickson.

The kinetoscope worked on the same basic principle as the phonograph, in that it turned on a hand crank and spun a wax cylinder that played sound; there was a second cylinder containing dozens of miniscule, hand-mounted photographs that passed beneath the lens of something like a microscope ocular, and when the device functioned properly, the music and pictures moved in sync. It was a clever device, but Edison wanted it to perform along the same lines as a color television set, which it could not do. Dickson was put in charge of preparing an advanced version of the kinetoscope in time for the Columbia Exposition, but all he managed to do was work himself into such a state of exhaustion that he had to stop work entirely. The kinetoscope would not be finished until nearly a year after the exposition was over.

Stross evaluates Edison's attitude towards the kinetoscope as follows:

"It was clear to everyone but Edison that the kinetoscope, once it was finally ready for release, would be a tremendous source of fun of all kinds—the silly, the spectacular, and the ribald. Even before the kinetoscope was released, an Albany newspaper reported on rumors that it would be perfectly suited for recording a boxing match, permitting hundreds of thousands to witness a match within a week after the event. Edison, however, continued to lecture the public in a churchy voice about the machine's suitability for performances at the Metropolitan Opera House in New York."

The kinetoscope and movie projectors

It had often been remarked of Edison that he knew very little about fun as most people understood the word. For him, work was fun—he took genuine delight in inventing, which explains a great deal about his 18 hour workdays. Fortunately for the future of entertainment, however, Dickson and Edison's other lab assistants knew a little more about how the average person had their fun. After building one of the first proto movie studios in Edison's laboratory, a haphazard construction nicknamed "Black Maria" after the police carriages of the day, they shot several short films for the kinetoscope. The first depicted a strongman showing off his muscles (his normal appearance fee was two hundred and fifty dollars, but he agreed to waive it if he was given the opportunity to shake hands with the famous inventor, Thomas Edison). The next film was of a Spanish dancer showing off a scandalous amount of leg, and the third film depicted a cockfight.

The kinetoscopes were soon installed in shops, and customers purchased tickets for the privilege of peering into the rubber tubes and watching the show, just as if they were attending the theater. Eventually, the machines were outfitted with coin slots, becoming the first coin operated entertainment devices, the great-grandmothers of arcade games. The coin operated kinetoscopes made an extraordinary profit, and they soon attracted the interest of two young men by the name of Grey and Otway Latham, and their friend Enoch Rector, who approached Edison's people in April of 1894 with an offer: they wanted to work with the technology of the kinetoscope to film and exhibit boxing matches.

The technology of the era limited the stories the kinetoscope's creators were able to tell with their machine—it could only play one twenty second reel at a time, and even when several kinetoscopes were placed in a row to form a longer narrative arc, it wasn't really possible to creative a full length story. But Enoch Rector managed to expand the kinetoscope's capacity from twenty second reels to sixty second reels, which could contain a three minute boxing match if the film were sped up a little. (One of the prize fighters who was invited to fight a match before Edison's cameras remarked that he could have hit his opponent faster, but he didn't want to move too fast for Edison's machine to keep up.) When the fight was exhibited in 1895, each of its six rounds was exhibited in a different machine; customers paid ten cents to see a single round and sixty to see all of them. The lines to view the kinetoscopes was so long that the police had to be called in to keep the crowd under control.

Edison was at this time principally occupied by his iron ore mining experiments in Ogden, and while he approved of the work his laboratory had done on the kinetoscope, he was less interested in the next big idea everyone had for improving it. Demand for the kinetoscopes was so high that Dickson, the Lathams, Rector, and the rest all realized that they could make far more money if they find a way to get the pictures out of the box and onto a screen. The kinetoscopes were boxes about four or five feet tall, with a set of eye holes for peeping in at the picture—customers had to remain on their feet, crouching awkwardly, in order to take in the show. If audiences could remain seated during a show, even more people would be interested in buying tickets, and if the picture could be projected on a central screen, tickets could be sold to as many people as the room could hold. Edison was not interested in developing a projector—he didn't think it could be done without compromising the quality of the pictures.

But other inventors were working on the projector behind Edison's back. The problem with the image quality came from the amount of time it took for light to pass through an image. The Latham brothers solved the problem by making the images wider, which produced the projector machine they called the pantoptikon. It was renamed the Eidoloscope shortly after, when it began to give public showings of "life sized" prize fights—drawing huge audiences. (Boxing was illegal in New Jersey and several other states; Edison had narrowly escaped being deposed over his role in filming a prize fight on his property. No doubt the illicit thrill contributed a great deal to ticket sales.) The most important adjustment to image quality came at the hands of two inventors named Francis Armat and C. Francis Jenkins, who realized that the light needed more time to pass through the images; their version of the projector, the Phantascope, paused each frame of the image so that the light could saturate it, resulting in a much clearer projection onto the screen.

It was Armat and Jenkin's "screen machine" that was ultimately marketed under Edison's name. His investors had begged him to invent a projector of his own, but he had reacted with about the same level of enthusiasm he had always shown when his investors were asking him to do things that clashed with his interest of the moment. He did, however, agree that it should be sold under the Edison brand, which was a first in his life—never before had he allowed someone else's improvement on one of his inventions to bear his name, though the American Graphophone Company had once made him a similar offer. The machine was finally made known to the public under the name of the vitascope.

In 1897, Edison appeared as the star of a twenty second film reel, called *Mr. Edison At Work In His Chemical Laboratory,* produced in the Black Maria studio. He spent the whole film rushing around the fake laboratory set as if he was very busily working on an experiment. It is probably safe to assume that contemporary audiences, being entirely new to the idea of films, did not quite realize that the laboratory was staged, or that Edison was not actually at work on any sort of experiment while he was on camera. Even if the average viewer had been more familiar with the film making process, they had no reason to question what they were seeing. In the reel,

Edison wears an enormous white lab coat, and he never looks at the camera—he's too busy moving fake chemicals from one table to the next, arranging them over burners, and studying the results with a pensive expression. The image he creates of himself, that of the distracted genius busily at work on arcane scientific matters the average person could not hope to understand, was exactly in keeping with the image he had always presented to the newspapers. It was a splendid piece of propaganda, and it goes a long way towards explaining the enduring legacy of his fame.

Chapter Eight: The Edison Name

"The public's interest in Thomas Edison's inventions rose and fell, as announcements of coming wonders would pique interest and then delays in the delivery of those wonders would disappoint. Over time, however, his fame acquired an indestructible sheath and eclipsed the attention accorded to the individual inventions themselves. It was Thomas Edison, the person, to whom the public became most attached during his lifetime. Edison realized this, and working unceasingly to protect the most distilled expression of his person: his name. 'Thomas A. Edison' was an estimable invention too."

Randall Stross, *The Wizard of Menlo Park*

Fake Edisons

If Edison's most effective invention was his own celebrity, it was just as susceptible as his other inventions to being purloined by opportunists. By the late 1890's, Edison was selling the rights to his name to manufacturers of a variety of clever inventions that he approved of, but had had no hand in inventing, for the simple reason that machines—or anything else—with the Edison name attached to it sold well. But there were other people named Edison in the world, and some of them discovered that they could sell the rights to their names to product manufacturers who were betting on the fact that the public would not inquire too deeply as to whether the Edison endorsing their product was, in fact, the famous inventor. Thomas Edison brought suit against these fake Edisons, which put a temporary stop to the fakery, but soon he was facing competition from a startling source: his own son.

Thomas Alva Edison, Jr., known as Junior to his family, wanted to be an inventor like his father. As the second child of Edison's first marriage, he had seen little of his father when he was a young boy, and even less of him after Mary Edison's death and Edison's remarriage. He attended boarding school as a teenager, but left without graduating because he was eager to begin his own career as an inventor. Edison had given him jobs at his West Orange laboratory and at the Ogden mining site, but Tom Edison was never able to find the kind of easy rapprochement with his father that he longed for. One wonders whether it was Edison's deafness which prevented them from communicating easily, or merely Tom's shyness. He seems to have had a cordial relationship with his step-mother, Mina, however, and he wrote her a letter in May of 1897 from the Ogden camp that expressed some of the frustration he felt in his famous father's company:

"My dear Mother—I was in hopes—'though I may not say how much'—that you would favor me with a word or two—it is true—I have only been away from 'Glenmont' a few days—but these days—Oh! How long they seem—I shall patiently wait—with that feeling of supreme content—and that feeling of certain expectancy—which some times comes over one—though to me this is rare—I will await those kind words that are indeed dearer—far dearer to me—than their author has ever—or will ever realize.

"But why should I ask you for your own words—knowing well I am not worth of a single one? Because it is you—I ask, mother, and no one else in this world—and no mother—has the heart to deprive her son of her words of advice and of her wisdom. Fortunately father has given me some work to lay out that greatly pleases me and I am hard at it—and I sincerely hope it will please him—which I am doing my level best to do-though I probably never will be able to please him—as I am afraid it is not in me.

"But I shall never give up trying—if I could only talk to him the way I want to—perhaps everything may be different. I have many ideas of my own which sometimes, yes, I may say on all occasions, I would like to ask him, or tell him about, but they never leave my mouth, and are soon forgotten—perhaps where they belong, perhaps not. This I would like to have him to decide—well, mother—I have no desire to bother you any longer—but I thought I would do as I deem it quite necessary—though unimportant that you should know that I still exist—and am thinking of those I love—as I always do."

Later that year, a reporter at the *New York Herald* wrote a profile of Tom entitled "Edison Jr., Wizard", which contained a number of grandiose assertions about his career as an inventor that played neatly into the Edison narrative but had no basis in fact, such as the claim that he had invented an incandescent light bulb far superior to his father's. The reporter accepted Tom's assertions without doing any research to back them up; the result was that he became an overnight celebrity in his own right. He was invited to be the celebrity guest of honor at the Electrical Exhibition at Madison Square Garden in 1898, and the public was allowed to assume that he was responsible for the electric light display they were seeing. In fact, his only job was to come up with a decorative design for the lights' arrangement; the promoters of the event merely wanted to be able to say than Edison had endorsed the exhibition. Tom was well paid for his involvement, but an even more lucrative opportunity awaited him.

Tom Edison began to be approached by investors who wanted to form companies of their own with his name attached. First was the Edison Jr. Steel and Iron Process Company, then the Thomas A. Edison, Jr. and William Holzer Steel and Iron Process Company. Tom was given a third of the shares from the first company and was made vice president of the second, but both companies went bankrupt quite quickly. Tom complained that he could not get loans from the banks because as soon as the bankers heard his name, they assumed that he could not possibly be in need of money—wasn't his famous father ludicrously wealthy already? Tom wrote accusingly to his father that if he had any competence as a businessman, or had left his business affairs to be managed by persons better suited to the task, he would have been a millionaire "ten times over". As it was, while the Edison family was fairly well off, Tom was anything but a spoiled trust fund baby.

After Tom's business endeavors ended in disgrace, with him being hounded from the city by debt collectors, he was approached by Edison

Chemical Company, which produced ink for commercial printers. Edison Chemical was named after a man by the name of C.M. Edison who had nothing to offer the company except being the namesake of the famous inventor. They had been forced out of business temporarily by a lawsuit from Thomas Edison, but that did not stop them from offering a deal to Thomas Jr.—it was one thing to deceive the public into the belief that their line of products had been endorsed by Edison, but what if they could legitimately tell the public that their products had been endorsed by his son? Tom was happy to accept the offer, not only because he needed the money, but because he finally had inventions of his own that he wanted to introduce to the public—including the "Magno Electric Vitalizer", which purported to cure any number of mysterious illnesses.

Predictably, Edison took the rebranded Thomas A. Edison, Jr. Chemical Company to court, and he won his case again. He made a number of unkind remarks about his son in the process, claiming that he had no abilities as an inventor whatsoever. Tom, for his part, crumbled swiftly under the force of his father's anger, and accepted a lump payment from him in exchange for never selling the rights to his name again—in fact, he briefly changed his name to Thomas Willard, as if feeling that he had relinquished all rights to being an Edison. So furious was Edison Sr. over the whole affair that he wrote to Tom's younger brother, instructing him to tell Tom that he didn't want to see him again. The harshness of this paternal judgment seemed to have a severe effect on Edison's oldest son, who would struggle for the rest of his life with alcohol and depression.

The music and automotive industries

There were two projects that chiefly absorbed Edison's interest in the late 1890's and early 1900's: one was related to music, and the other to car batteries. The latter was his priority.

Edison was hard at work upon designing a battery that would power an electric car; he anticipated that it would be less expensive for the average person than keeping a horse. At the same time, improvements in phonograph technology were giving birth to the rise of the recorded music industry. Victor and Columbia, still titans of the music industry today, got their start when it was discovered that disc shaped records could hold twice the amount of music as the original phonograph cylinder (four minutes, rather than two.) For the first time, musicians were recording their work and achieving fame and money through sales of their songs. The single thus predated the album, as it would be many years before recording technology was capable of storing more than one song on a record at a time.

One could be forgiven for supposing that a man with Edison's hearing impairments would not have much opinion of music. He could hear music, but only with difficulty; he remarked to one newspaper that when he listened to the phonograph, he had to place his ear directly against the wooden cabinet, and if that didn't work, he had to sink his teeth into the wood to catch the vibrations traveling through his mouth. He had many opinions about music, however—in fact, Edison had opinions about everything, and never hesitated to set himself up as an expert in any field that captured his interest, or that was related, however incidentally, to his inventions. Edison had very clear ideas about what sort of music was worth recording and selling and what sort of music was beneath him, and by extension, beneath his company. His standards for music were idiosyncratic; he detested jazz, but he also disliked some composers performing in the hallowed halls of classical music performance, like Sergei Rachmaninoff. He claimed, somewhat eccentrically, that all true music lovers preferred "soft" music, and that only consumers of "soft music" were likely to be repeat, loyal customers of phonograph records—those who preferred jazz or other such "fads" were bound to be one time customers, incapable of sustaining the recording industry as a whole.

In fact, the rules of success in the music business were the same in the 1890's as they are today: certain songs become hits, resulting in huge sales for a brief period of time. The sales from a handful of successful songs paid for the hundreds of other releases that did not achieve meteoric fame. Edison had never displayed much understanding of the market forces that directed the sales of his invention—he had a lifelong habit of clinging stubbornly to his own idea of how consumers *ought* to behave, just as when he insisted that the phonograph was more useful as an office tool for taking dictation than as an entertainment device. He was particularly irritated by the celebrity complex that sprung up around musical performers who made contracts with the phonograph companies; perhaps reflecting his irritability with his own fame, he felt that attention paid to the performer was only a distraction from the attention that ought to be paid to the music. He tried to forbid the record companies from attaching the names of the performers to the records of their songs. But the era of the celebrity musician was upon him, and he could not hold out against it for long.

Henry Ford

One of the consequences of Edison's fame was that he did not have many close friends. He was naturally suspicious of the motivations of anyone who approached him, especially if they were also businessmen or had interests in technology and invention. He felt that he had been betrayed in the past by people who used their personal connections with him to make private deals injurious to his interests, which probably explains why he was so upset over the debacle with Tom Jr. and thc Edison Chcmical Company. In order to strike up a true friendship with someone, that person had to be his equal—

someone with whom he had interests in common, but who was successful enough in their own right not to need anything from him, in terms of his celebrity or his technology. When Edison was in his sixties, such a person appeared to him in the form of Henry Ford, inventor of the Model T car.

Ford was sixteen years Edison's junior, and he had idolized Edison since he was a young man, working for one of Edison's electric light companies. They met once, before Ford was famous, at a conference in Michigan. Ford was giving a lecture outlining his plan for the internal combustion engine. According to Ford, Edison was so interested in the lecture that he traded seats with someone closer to the front of the room so that he could hear better, and after asking a lot of questions, declared that Ford had hit upon the secret to making cars cheap and accessible. Edison was notorious for refusing to give encouragement to other inventors, or even acknowledge when they had a good idea, so this praise, coming from his idol, affected Ford deeply. Ford credited Edison's encouragement with giving him the inspiration to push forward until the internal combustion engine was completed.

They did not meet for a second time until 1912, after the Model T was in production and Ford was nearly as famous as Edison was. Ford negotiated with Edison's secretaries for months until Edison agreed to let him pay a visit to his laboratory; from that point forward, they were fast friends. Ford, knowing of Edison's interest in electric cars, asked him to design an electrical system for Ford automobiles. Edison replied that he would be very interested in such a project, but that he could not afford to finance it privately— he could go to Wall Street in search of investors, but he was afraid that his credit with the business world was long spent. Ford was himself deeply antagonistic towards Wall Street, and his personal affection and admiration for Edison was such that he instantly volunteered to become Edison's financial partner in the battery development scheme.

Being famous and busy men, Edison and Ford did not have much time to socialize in person, but in the last decades of his life, Edison probably saw more of Ford than he did of anyone else who was not a member of his own family or an employee in his workshop. Their families took vacations together, and Ford showered the Edisons with presents—he sent them dozens of cars from his factories and dealerships, not only to Edison himself, but to his sons. At this point in Edison's career, he did not have much to offer Ford except for friendship and approval—advantage in the friendship flowed almost entirely from Ford to Edison, not the other way around.

This became manifestly obvious over time, as the electric battery Edison was working on for the Ford company failed to work. Edison had, as usual, split his attention from the battery project to work on the phonograph, but even when he made the batteries his priority, no working model resulted. The most remarkable result of Ford and Edison's business collaboration was that their personal friendship endured despite its failure. Ford seems not have been surprised that Edison was unable to deliver on his promises, or to have minded when Edison was unable to repay his loans on schedule. After a disastrous fire in Edison's laboratory, Ford gave him a hundred thousand dollars to rebuild; and in 1925, when Edison's health was failing, Ford forgave the outstanding balance of all his business loans.

Ford famously remarked that Edison was the best inventor in the world, and the worst businessman—because he did not know or care anything about business. It was an observation made of Edison many times in his life, but from Ford, the criticism was affectionate. In his eyes, Edison deserved every honor solely on the basis of his skill as an inventor. His business failures did not detract from his brilliance in any way. Edison and Ford saw more, not less of each other after their business collaboration came to a disappointing end.

Edison's final years

Edison experienced poor health in his declining years; he had diabetes, and he had stomach problems of an undiagnosed nature that may have been the result of early, dangerous experiments with x-rays (his assistant in the x-ray experiments had developed skin cancer as a result, suffering amputation of his arm before meeting an early death.) However, even though he gave his sons Charles and Theodore positions of limited responsibility in Thomas A. Edison, Inc., he was not willing to step away and turn the business over to them. To the end of his life, he believed he was just on the verge of his next world-changing breakthrough.

In 1915, with the United States on the verge of joining World War I, Edison was asked to join the newly formed Naval Consulting Board, in which civilian scientists proposed technological innovations that would give the U.S. navy strategic advantages in warfare. Edison placed himself fully at the board's disposal. Aboard the U.S.S. *Sachem*, a private yacht purchased by the navy just for Edison's experiments, he investigated the potential of various machines that could help camouflage the positions of ships and guns, and detect the positions of torpedoes. According to the U.S. Park Service, "Edison would spend eighteen months in the field, and would conceive of a total of forty-eight different projects, including a hydrogen-detecting alarm to avert the danger of undersea explosions, vaseline and zinc antirust coating for submarine guns, and an antiroll platform for ships' to ensure accuracy in rough seas." His military consulting career left him dissatisfied, however, as the navy ultimately did not implement a single one of his inventions. This was not a personal slight against Edison, however; of the nearly one thousand ideas fielded by the Naval Consulting Board, only about a hundred were ever considered for serious implementation by the navy, and only one of those actual came to be used in the war.

During Edison's war time service, his son Charles, as the acting head of the company, created a new personnel department, the goal of which was to improve the lives of the laborers in Edison's factories. He shortened the work day from twelve hours to ten hours, and founded an on-site infirmary staffed by a doctor and a nurse in the case of workplace accidents; he even instituted a workman's compensation program, against advice that doing so might bankrupt the company. However, after the war, Edison took full control of the company again and eliminated all the changes Charles had made. When the company began to suffer losses during the Great Depression, he singlehandedly fired seven thousand of the company's ten thousand employees. According to legend, he would walk down the halls of a company and confront employees with abrupt questions about the nature of their duties; if they did not reply to his satisfaction, he fired them on the spot.

In 1929, when Edison was eighty two, the incandescent light bulb celebrated its fiftieth anniversary. An enormous celebration, Light's Golden Jubilee, was arranged by Henry Ford, and included such famous guests as President Herbert Hoover, scientist Marie Curie, inventor of the airplane Orville Wright, and billionaires John D. Rockefeller Jr. and J.P. Morgan. A special ceremony was broadcast live on radio, in which Edison, accompanied by Ford and Hoover, re-enacted the moment that the first incandescent bulb flickered into life. "Mr. Edison has two wires in his hand," said the broadcaster narrating the event. "Now he is reaching up to the old lamp, now he is making the connection. It lights! Light's Golden Jubilee has come to a triumphant climax!"

Edison lived for another two years after this ceremony. In January of 1931 he filed his final patent, bringing the total of patents filed over the course of his career to one thousand and ninety three. Later that year, he suffered kidney failure, only to recover for another few months. Finally, October 18, 1931, after spending several weeks in bed in an intermittent coma, Thomas Edison died at home at Glenmont, the house he had purchased for a steal forty years earlier as a wedding gift for his wife Mina. He was surrounded by his wife and family.

The day of Edison's death, his obituary appeared in the *New York Times* under the title, "Human Qualities of the Inventor and Varied Aspects of His Busy Life Recalled":

"Thomas Alva Edison made the world a better place in which to live and brought comparative luxury into the life of the workingman. No one in the long roll of those who have benefited humanity has done more to make existence easy and comfortable. Through his invention of electric light he gave the world a new brilliance; when the cylinder of his first phonograph recorded sound he put the great music of the ages within reach of every one; when he invented the motion picture it was a gift to mankind of a new theatre, a new form of amusement. His inventions gave work as well as light and recreation to millions.

"His inventive genius brooded over a world which at nightfall was engulfed in darkness, pierced only by the feeble beams of kerosene lamps, by gas lights or, in some of the larger cities, by the uncertainties of the old-time arc lights. To Edison, with the dream of the incandescent lamp in his mind, it seemed that people still lived in the Dark Ages. But his ferreting fingers groped in the darkness until they evoked the glow that told him the incandescent lamp was a success, and that light for all had been achieved.

"Thus he permitted others to carry on his pioneering in this fertile field, but it is because of his early discoveries that America leads the world in screen effects, and that the penny arcade, with its shooting gallery and knockout fight films, has yielded to the cathedrals of the screen. Also, because of Edison, it is possible for the natives of Kamchatka to sit impassively, row upon row, and see how the high school champion diving team of Rural Centre, Ill., put on a water carnival and raised money to pay the church mortgage. And vice versa, for the students of Rural Centre to see what the well-controlled native of Bengal does when a hungry tiger charges him. Edison did more than light the lamp at Menlo Park."

Other books available by Michael W. Simmons on Kindle, paperback and audio:

Nikola Tesla: Prophet Of The Modern Technological Age

Albert Einstein: Father Of the Modern Scientific Age

Alexander Hamilton: First Architect of the American Government

Appendix A: Edison's Employment Exam

The following test was administered to all employees seeking a job with Edison's company. Once considered the ultimate barometer of intelligence, it came to be printed in magazines and newspapers, whose readers would take the test as a game. Edison admitted that he used it to weed out college graduates who lacked practical experience. Amusingly, Edison's own son, Theodore, who studied physics at the Massachusetts Institute of Technology, failed the test—but Edison reportedly assured him that he would hire him anyway.

1. What countries bound France?

2. What city and country produce the finest china?

3. Where is the River Volga?

4. What is the finest cotton grown?

5. What country consumed the most tea before the war?

6. What city in the United States leads in making laundry machines?

7. What city is the fur centre of the United States?

8. What country is the greatest textile producer?

9. Is Australia greater than Greenland in area?

10. Where is Copenhagen?

11. Where is Spitzbergen?

12. In what country other than Australia are kangaroos found?

13. What telescope is the largest in the world?

14. Who was Bessemer and what did he do?

15. How many states in the Union?

16. Where do we get prunes from?

17. Who was Paul Revere?

18. Who was John Hancock?

19. Who was Plutarch?

20. Who was Hannibal?

21. Who was Danton?

22. Who was Solon?

23. Who was Francis Marion?

24. Who was Leonidas?

25. Where did we get Louisiana from?

26. Who was Pizarro?

27. Who was Bolivar?

28. What war material did Chile export to the Allies during the war?

29. Where does most of the coffee come from?

30. Where is Korea?

31. Where is Manchuria?

32. Where was Napoleon born?

33. What is the highest rise of tide on the North American Coast?

34. Who invented logarithms?

35. Who was the Emperor of Mexico when Cortez landed?

36. Where is the Imperial Valley and what is it noted for?

37. What and where is the Sargasso Sea?

38. What is the greatest known depth of the ocean?

39. What is the name of a large inland body of water that has no outlet?

40. What is the capital of Pennsylvania?

41. What state is the largest? Next?

42. Rhode Island is the smallest state. What is the next and the next?

43. How far is it from New York to Buffalo?

44. How far is it from New York to San Francisco?

45. How far is it from New York to Liverpool?

46. Of what state is Helena the capital?

47. Of what state is Tallahassee the capital?

48. What state has the largest copper mines?

49. What state has the largest amethyst mines?

50. What is the name of a famous violin maker?

51. Who invented the modern paper-making machine?

52. Who invented the typesetting machine?

53. Who invented printing?

54. How is leather tanned?

55. What is artificial silk made from?

56. What is a caisson?

57. What is shellac?

58. What is celluloid made from?

59. What causes the tides?

60. To what is the change of the seasons due?

61. What is coke?

62. From what part of the North Atlantic do we get codfish?

63. Who reached the South Pole?

64. What is a monsoon?

65. Where is the Magdalena Bay?

66. From where do we import figs?

67. From where do we get dates?

68. Where do we get our domestic sardines?

69. What is the longest railroad in the world?

70. Where is Kenosha?

71. What is the speed of sound?

72. What is the speed of light?

73. Who was Cleopatra and how did she die?

74. Where are condors found?

75. Who discovered the law of gravitation?

76. What is the distance between the earth and sun?

77. Who invented photography?

78. What country produces the most wool?

79. What is felt?

80. What cereal is used in all parts of the world?

81. What states produce phosphates?

82. Why is cast iron called pig iron?

83. Name three principal acids?

84. Name three powerful poisons.

85. Who discovered radium?

86. Who discovered the X-ray?

87. Name three principal alkalis.

88. What part of Germany do toys come from?

89. What States bound West Virginia?

90. Where do we get peanuts from?

91. What is the capital of Alabama?

92. Who composed "Il Trovatore"?

93. What is the weight of air in a room 20 by 30 by 10?

94. Where is platinum found?

95. With what metal is platinum associated when found?

96. How is sulphuric acid made?

97. Where do we get sulphur from?

98. Who discovered how to vulcanize rubber?

99. Where do we import rubber from?

100. What is vulcanite and how is it made?

101. Who invented the cotton gin?

102. What is the price of 12 grains of gold?

103. What is the difference between anthracite and bituminous coal?

104. Where do we get benzol from?

105. Of what is glass made?

106. How is window glass made?

107. What is porcelain?

108. What country makes the best optical lenses and what city?

109. What kind of a machine is used to cut the facets of diamonds?

110. What is a foot pound?

111. Where do we get borax from?

112. Where is the Assuan Dam?

113. What star is it that has been recently measured and found to be of enormous size?

114. What large river in the United States flows from south to north?

115. What are the Straits of Messina?

116. What is the highest mountain in the world?

117. Where do we import cork from?

118. Where is the St. Gothard tunnel?

119. What is the Taj Mahal?

120. Where is Labrador?

121. Who wrote "The Star-Spangled Banner"?

122. Who wrote "Home, Sweet Home"?

123. Who was Martin Luther?

124. What is the chief acid in vinegar?

125. Who wrote "Don Quixote"?

126. Who wrote "Les Miserables"?

127. What place is the greatest distance below sea level?

128. What are axe handles made of?

129. Who made "The Thinker"?

130. Why is a Fahrenheit thermometer called Fahrenheit?

131. Who owned and ran the New York Herald for a long time?

132. What is copra?

133. What insect carries malaria?

134. Who discovered the Pacific Ocean?

135. What country has the largest output of nickel in the world?

136. What ingredients are in the best white paint?

137. What is glucose and how made?

138. In what part of the world does it never rain?

139. What was the approximate population of England, France, Germany and Russia before the war?

140. Where is the city of Mecca?

141. Where do we get quicksilver from?

142. Of what are violin strings made?

143. What city on the Atlantic seaboard is the greatest pottery centre?

144. Who is called the "father of railroads" in the United States?

145. What is the heaviest kind of wood?

146. What is the lightest wood?

Further Reading

The Wizard of Menlo Park, by Randall Stross

Nikola Tesla: Man Out of Time, by Margaret Cheney

Edison: His Life and Inventions, by Frank Lewis Dyer

>http://www.iar.unicamp.br/lab/luz/ld/History%F3ria/Edison%20His%20Life%20and%20Inventions.pdf

"The Talking Phonograph", *Scientific American,* December 22, 1877

>http://www.phonozoic.net/n0027.htm

"Edison's Improved Phonograph", *New York World,* November 18, 1878

>http://www.phonozoic.net/n0042.htm

"A Marvelous Discovery", *New York Sun*, 1878

http://edison.rutgers.edu/NamesSearch/SingleDoc.php3?DocId=MBSB10378

"A Food Creator", *New York Daily Graphic,* April 1, 1878

> http://fultonhistory.com/Newspaper%2011/New%20York%20NY%20Daily%20Graphic/New%20York%20NY%20Daily%20Graphic%201878%20Jan-Jun%20Grayscale/New%20York%20NY%20Daily%20Graphic%201878%20Jan-Jun%20Grayscale%20-%200651.pdf

Op-ed from *The Brooklyn Daily Eagle,* November 26, 1878

> http://bklyn.newspapers.com/image/50424106

"Edison's Light", *New York Herald,* December 21, 1879

> http://edison.rutgers.edu/NamesSearch/DocDetImage.php3

"A New Use for Electricity", *New York Times,* January 12, 1882 http://query.nytimes.com/mem/archive-free/pdf?res=950DE3D6153BE033A25751C1A9679C94639FD7CF

"Thomas Edison's First Wife May Have Died of A Morphine Overdose"

http://news.rutgers.edu/research-news/thomas-edison%E2%80%99s-first-wife-may-have-died-morphine-overdose/20111115#.V4R6JOYrJE4

"The Diary of Thomas Alva Edison"

http://ariwatch.com/VS/TheDiaryOfThomasEdison.htm

"Struck Dead In A Second", *New York Times*, January 21, 1887

http://query.nytimes.com/mem/archive-free/pdf?res=9A00E6D81639E233A25752C2A9679C94669FD7CF

"To Abolish Hanging", *New York Times*, January 23, 1887

http://query.nytimes.com/mem/archive-free/pdf?res=980DE6DA163AE033A25757C2A9679C94669FD7CF

"Thomas Edison in World War I"

https://www.nps.gov/edis/learn/historyculture/thomas-edison-in-world-war-i.htm

Made in the USA
Monee, IL
23 September 2019